to: Norman & Anya

With my best wishes.

Carla O. Peperzak

Keys of My

Life

A Memoir by

Carla Olman

Peperzak

Respect

Remember

Keys of My Life,
A Memoir by Carla Olman Peperzak
Biography / Memoir / Jewish History / Holocaust
ISBN-13: 978-1-937207-28-1
© 2018 Carla Olman Peperzak
Creating Calm Network Publishing Group
Back cover author's photo credit: Rick Singer Photography

Keys of My Life

A Memoir by Carla Olman Peperzak

"The piano keys are black and white but they sound like a million colors in your mind"

— Maria Cristina Mena,
The Collected Stories of Maria Cristina Mena

Acknowledgements

It has taken me 18 years to write down all these memories. If it wasn't for my daughter, Yvonne, the memories would still be in my bookcase on paper written in long hand. She spent countless hours typing this manuscript, talking on the phone with me, and talking to her sisters, Marian and Joan along with flying to Spokane numerous times. Without her, there would be no book. It is hard to express sufficient gratitude to her.

I am grateful to daughter, Marian, she was a great help in getting facts straight and spent many hours editing. I am also deeply grateful to Marian who is always ready to be my chauffeur and guide and computer wizard for my presentations to schools on my experiences during the Holocaust. I truly could not do this without her help and encouragement.

My daughter, Joan, offered good suggestions and feedback. She also provided morale support and a lot of encouragement, as have my son, Marc and his wife Karen.

My son Marc and his wife Karen's gave me a lot of encouragement. And my granddaughter, Julie, assisted by making and sending photos of the piano. I appreciate my friend, Sue Lindenberg's help. I also wish to thank Lisa VanMansum, Rockwood's communications coordinator for all the hours she spent doing the final corrections. And last, but far from least, was the publisher who made the book a reality, Kimberly Burnham.

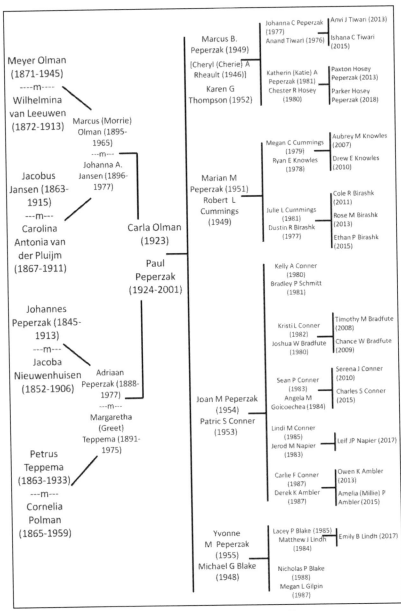

Carla and Paul Peperzak's Family

"She carried the toddler off the train. But the station was teeming with German soldiers, and a couple of them stopped her. Who are you and where are you going, they wanted to know.

Carla Olman Peperzak was a teenage wartime Dutch Resistance operative who, by her estimation, helped hide approximately 40 Jews from the Germans during World War II. She forged identification papers for about five dozen others, served as a messenger for the Underground movement and helped publish a newsletter of Allied Forces' activities on a banned mimeograph machine.

These are not the things she told the Nazis." — Spokesman Review (Jan 25, 2015) in Freedom fighter: Spokane's Carla Peperzak protected fellow Jews through Dutch Resistance during World War II.

http://www.spokesman.com/stories/2015/jan/25/freedom -fighter/

At Paul and Carla's 50th Wedding Anniversary
at the Broadmoor Hotel in Colorado Springs – November 1997.

Dedication

I wish to dedicate this book to my offspring: my four children (my son Marc and his wife Karen Thompson, my daughter Marian and her husband, Bob Cummings, my daughter Joan and her husband Pat Conner, my daughter Yvonne and her husband Michael Blake); to my eleven grandchildren and currently seventeen great grandchildren (my granddaughter Johanna Peperzak and husband Anand Tiwari and their two daughters, Anvi and Ishana; my granddaughter, Katie Peperzak and husband Chet Hosey and their sons, Paxton and Parker; my granddaughter Megan Cummings and husband Ryan Knowles and their children Aubrey and Drew; my granddaughter Julie

9

Cummings and husband Dustin Birashk and children Cole, Rose and Ethan; my granddaughter Kelly Conner and husband Brad Schmitt; my granddaughter Kristi Conner and husband Josh Bradfute and sons Timothy and Chance; my grandson Sean Conner and wife Angela and children Serena and Charles; my granddaughter Lindi Conner and husband Jerod Napier and son Leif; my granddaughter Carlie Conner and husband Derek Ambler and children Owen and Amelia; my granddaughter Lacey Blake and husband Matthew Lindh and daughter Emily and my youngest grandchild Nicholas Blake and his wife Megan Gilpin). I also dedicate this book to my extended family and to the many good friends and wonderful people, who influenced my life over the many years.

Papa's piano.

Contents

"Thank you so much for coming to our River City Middle School AP English Class. It was such an honor to have someone like you with your story to come and speak to the class. You helped inspire me greatly when writing the essay. When you told us all of the stories, you brought so much awareness of this tragedy into our school and we want to thank you very much for that. You gave us so many useful tips to handle our problems. I would like to thank you again for coming to our school to speak."

—Mikayla Melchert, Post Falls Middle School, 2013.

Carla Olman 1947, Amsterdam.

Remembering

Many months have passed since I started and last worked on my memoir. It is February 2018. During the last five or six years I have been talking about my experiences during the Holocaust – mainly to students at universities, high schools, middle schools and a few grade schools. In my view, it is very important to let people and, especially young people, know what really happened during the Holocaust. The more informed they are, the better they can understand that terrible time and, hopefully, prevent it from happening again.

For many years the Holocaust survivors did not talk about what happened. Most of us wanted to live a normal life and forget about the atrocities. Of course, forgetting was impossible! Only in the last 15 to 20 years have survivors started to talk.

The result of this silence is that several generations of young people have no clue what happened. This was brought home to me last week watching the documentary "The Last Laugh." Towards the second half of the movie, some of the younger generations' comedians think they are funny if they tell a joke about the Holocaust. I was shocked to the core of my being. I am so sad that 75 years later people feel they can do this. The memory of six million Jews killed only because they were Jews, does not mean anything any longer? How can that be? It made me realize how important it is to continue talking and explaining what happened during those awful years.

I was fortunate and very lucky to live through the war years unharmed. However, my life, and outlook on life, changed. I did not want to have any part of Judaism anymore. Also the memories were there and I tried to forget, but that was impossible. Even today, looking at pictures or a movie about the camps makes me want to cry. A nazie uniform gives me the chills.

I am asked if I can forgive. I cannot. Only God can forgive killers. How can I forgive those who killed so many of my uncles, aunts, cousins, nephews, nieces and friends because they were Jews?

Sometimes I am asked about Revenge. My personal revenge is sweet: To live a good, productive life, to have four children, eleven grandchildren and currently seventeen great grandchildren is very special and

something the nazies* never wanted to have happen. I am
so very grateful.

*This is the Dutch spelling of nazi and lower case is because I
don't want to give them the honor.

Carla's 90th Birthday at the Broadmoor Hotel in Colorado Springs, with most of the family in 2013 (prior to the birth of the following great grandchildren; Paxton, Charles, Amelia, Ishana, Ethan, Emily, Leif, and Parker.

My Keys to Life

It seems such a daunting task to start writing one's memoirs. Over the years I have been asked to do so. I've been working on them on and off (more off than on) for almost two decades.

I always feel good when I am busy with a project that involves other people. Life has to be meaningful for me. This does not mean only the big important things are meaningful, but the small every day things we do are important.

Life is not easy and everyone will encounter major problems through life. I firmly believe that it is not the problem itself, but how one reacts or acts toward the problem, which makes your life good or bad. My advice is to make the best of it by being positive and by trying to see the best in other people. Be "open" to life, accept it and at the same time try to improve it.

After my husband Paul died for the first year or so, I felt that life was not worth living, though there was no choice. I would not have minded to die. In fact, I wanted to.

I had never lived by myself. Before marriage, I was at home with my parents. After marriage, there was Paul and later the children. After the children left home and Paul would be away for weeks at a time, I always could look forward to his homecoming.

All that changed drastically after his passing. Being alone and the loneliness were very difficult. Even when I was with the kids or with friends, the loneliness was there. It still can hit me. However, I try not to let it get to me.

These are my wishes for my family. Of course, I wish for everyone to be healthy and not to have any money worries, but I wish more for the goodness in everyone to be shown to your families and the people around you. Do not be selfish, "live right" and live in "harmony." I wish all of you to keep in contact, to get together once in a while. If there is something you do not like; talk it over and try to understand each other. For families to be friends is maybe the most important thing. Try to love each other.

Paul said it best in his farewell letter to me. "*Even when everything seems hopeless and all is gone, love remains and love keeps us going. We were born in love and all our life we are seeking love, and once we depart from this life, we will return to the ultimate of LOVE, the love of God, our Creator."*

Real and true happiness may not be possible as long as we are alive. Paul's brother, Ad, said after Paul passed, *"He now knows true happiness."* One may be truly happy for brief periods of time, but then some problem may arise which makes life difficult and one's happiness is gone. I found the Indonesian word *Senang* comes closest to what I hope that all people can achieve. The way I interpret *Senang* is satisfaction with what one does, feeling good about yourself and consequently feeling good about the people around you.

Interesting enough my children were raised Catholic. I was Catholic, and of course, Paul was. God has always been important in my life. The path to God is different for each individual. For me, it was and is through Judaism. However, when the war started, being Jewish became such a tremendous burden, basically a death sentence; many of us gave it up altogether and wanted no part of it. Hence, I became a Catholic, though deep in my heart I never believed that Christ was God's son. I went through all the motions and I tried to reason and use my head, but my heart was never in it. I could never quite really believe all the things one was told to believe.

Over the years, when we were living in Kenya (we had stopped going to church, and the children were grown), it became harder and harder to accept the teachings of Christianity. My belief in God was there, but not all the other stuff. Slowly, but surely, Paul felt the same way. So we stopped going to church. Upon return to the States, we went several times to church, but the attitude of the priest toward the Jews was unacceptable to us. There were several times I wanted to walk out during a sermon. So, we stopped going to the Catholic Church. I always missed the temple and my association with Jewish people. When we lived in Colorado Springs, we met some people who went to the Reform temple and we joined the congregation. Initially, I went by myself; later Paul wanted to go with me. We did not go often; primarily we attended on the High Holy Days. I really started to feel at home again and I realized that this was what I wanted and needed.

As a young child, I had joined a Reform temple in Amsterdam. The rabbi was German. I still remember his name, Rabbi Mehler. Anne Frank and her sister, Margot, (who I knew well) also attended the same temple. I went to his house for Hebrew lessons when I was 13 or 14 years old. My parents did not seem to mind. They also did not encourage or disapprove so I never knew if they liked it or not.

*Carla's parents, Jo and Mor, her sister, Miep and Carla
in 1947-1948 before she left for the United States.*

Family Background

Every Friday night, dinner at home was a special meal with music and singing afterwards. Before dinner our hair was washed and my father dried it. The pickle man came by before dinner and my mother selected his best pickles. I loved those Friday evenings. Religion had really nothing to do with it. It was more about Tradition.

Talking about religion and religious preferences, I believe in God and for me the path is via Judaism. This makes the most sense to me. However, I also feel strongly that every person should do their own thing, whatever way each person chooses to live their life is up to them. It is far from me to push my will and my ethical outlook upon my children, grandchildren and great grandchildren. It would make me happy if someone chooses a Jewish spouse, but the most important thing in life is to be good, honest, true and responsible. I feel strongly that family matters very much and as I said earlier, I hope and pray that all of you will keep in touch with each other; and have a reunion once in a while. Families grow but it still should be possible to get together.

My paternal grandfather was Meyer Olman, born in Delft in 1865. He was a musician, an accomplished pianist, and a composer. He made his living by teaching and composing. For several years he played the piano and accompanied silent movies. He was quite a Bon Vivant. I understand my father's mother, Wilhelmina van Leeuwen, was deeply religious and had a kosher home. My grandfather could not care less. She died in childbirth when the seventh child, Eef, was born. I never knew my grandmother. My father was the eldest of their seven children followed by Eli, Ali, Ro, Dien, Lo, and Eef. Eli was born on December 31st and Lo was born on January 1st so before the war we would get together and celebrate each of their birthdays on New Years' Eve and New Year's Day – all at the same party! Eli, Ali and Eef, their spouses and children all perished in concentration camps during the war. My father, however, was fortunate to survive the war. He was detained several times, however, for reasons unknown to me; he managed to return home each time.

My father was 17 or 18 when his mother died. My grandfather could not take care of all seven children after

Wilhelmina died and they were placed among relatives. I believe they were separated because there were enough uncles and aunts to go around and take them in and take care of them. My father lived with the Cats' family. One of the children, Meyer Cats, was my father's best friend and they lived as brothers their entire lives. Meyer Cats later married Engeltje Trommel and they had one child, Jopie. Sadly, Engeltje, Jopie's mother, committed suicide by walking into the river following Jopie's birth. She had postpartum depression.

Carla's father, Marcus (Mordechai) Olman
born March 10, 1895 in Rotterdam, The Netherlands.

Engeltje was my mother's best friend. Engeltje's sister, Cor Trommel, married my father's brother, Eli Olman (my uncle). It is common for Jewish families to have multiple ties among families.

Engeltje's husband, Meyer Cats, remarried, moved to Argentina and had two more children (Zus Pais and Hans Cats). As a result, these two children were Argentinean citizens and received better treatment while being incarcerated in the camps during the Holocaust. The family had returned to Holland years before the War. In April 1945, when they were being shipped on a cattle car train to Auschwitz, the train was stopped because of allied bombing of the tracks. The Russian army liberated everyone on that train on April 17, 1945 and this became their liberation day.

Diamond Wedding Star.

The Diamond Star

The Diamond Star that all my granddaughters have worn at their weddings belonged to Tante Cor Olman Trommel; she was the wife of Eli, my father's brother (she and Eli and children all perished in the war). She was very orthodox. The nazies confiscated all the bank accounts, security accounts and safe deposit boxes of the Jewish people. The neighbors of those who were sent to camp or went into hiding often stole items from the vacated Jewish homes. Months after the war my father was notified about a Swiss bank account and safe deposit in the name of Eli Olman. My father, as next of kin, became the beneficiary. The diamond star was in the safe deposit box. My father gave it to my mother. And after she died the star was given to me. My father decided it could have been possible that Eli was killed before Cor, and in that case she would have inherited Eli's estate. Her only surviving relative was Jopie Markus Cats. My father made the decision to give the majority of Tante Cor and Oom Eli's inheritance to Jopie. Her husband, Jules Markus, used the money as start up for what became the only and highly successful chewing gum factory in The Netherlands. They named it Maple Leaf to honor Canada whose military liberated the northern part of the country.

To me the Diamond Star is precious and very important; it represents a victim of the Holocaust, a well-beloved uncle and aunt, the magic of family and the blessing to be alive. It has been my very special blessing to have seen all my granddaughters wear it on their wedding days.

It is my wish that all my female descendants wear the star at their weddings. Marian is the keeper of the diamond star. The responsibility of the star will be passed down to Megan, my granddaughter, than Aubrey, my great granddaughter, and down that lineage. It is my hope that when a family member marries they will contact Megan, Aubrey and descendants and wear the star at their wedding. This will ensure the family will stay in contact in the future.

Carla's mother, Jo Olman Jansen,
born August 3, 1896 in Rotterdam, The Netherlands.

Family Background Continues

My grandfather remarried about eight years after the death of Wilhelmina, to a non-Jewish woman. My father was not happy with this second marriage. My father and mother married around the same time in 1920. My grandfather's two children (Hennie and Kitty) by the second marriage were born around the same time as my sister, Miep Philips Olman and I.

Of the seven children in my father's family (three boys and four girls), only my father and two of his sisters married non-Jewish mates. When one of my aunts, Tante (Aunt) Ro, who died at 100 years of age in 2000, (she was born in 1900), dated a non-Jewish boy she was locked in an attic room. She jumped out of the window and broke her back! She recovered and later married that boy!

We were the only ones of the family who lived in Amsterdam, most stayed in Rotterdam; both my mother's siblings and my father's. Eventually Tante Eef, the youngest sister, moved to Zeist. Tante Ro moved to Indonesia with her Navy spouse. During the war the Japanese interned her and her two children, Wil and Leen, in Surabaya. Her husband was on a Dutch Naval ship when the Japanese invaded Indonesia. For four years they were unable to know if either had survived. They were all united after the war and moved back to Holland.

Tante Dien moved to Utrecht. Dien had two sons, Joop and Hans van Londen. Joop became a Medical Doctor (Psychiatrist) who for a number of years was in charge of the World Health Organization. We did try to get together with Tante Dien and Oom (Uncle) Jo van London (her husband) as often as possible. I always enjoyed our get-togethers. Before the war we often had the whole family together, usually for Sunday lunch.

I never knew my mother's parents, Johannes and Carolina Jansen. Johannes was a meat butcher. He supplied ocean liners with meat. My grandmother died in 1911 and my grandfather died in the flu epidemic in 1917. My mother was only 15 years old when her mother passed away. All five of the children were sent to an orphanage because my grandfather was unable to care for them. My mother never talked much about the orphanage. Actually, all she ever told me was that she had lived in the orphanage for a number of years. She hated priests for the rest of her life. Despite that experience she never objected to me becoming a Catholic during the war. She thought becoming a Catholic would keep me safe from the nazies.

When my mother was old enough, she was rescued from the orphanage by a Jewish family and became a housekeeper and part of the family. There she learned a lot about Jewish cooking and Jewish traditions. She met my father through that family.

My mother was closest to her sister, Lie (Caroline), and her brother Johan. The other sister, Ko, we saw maybe once a year and her brother, Anton, even less than that. He and his wife stole from my father during the war. Lie died rather young, her husband gave her a motor scooter on her 60th birthday, and she drove it out of the driveway, was hit and killed. Their only son, Jack de Groot, was my only cousin and close friend from that side of the family. He lived for awhile at my parents' home. Initially, he studied and entered the Merchant Marines. He left the merchant marines to work for my father. He enjoyed the fashion industry so much it became his chosen field.

Before the war, my father was always looking for a relative to take over his business and he talked Jack into learning the business. Jack learned well, he never took over my father's business. He, instead, went to Spain and Belgium after the war because of the activities he was involved in during and immediately after the war. He was a very active and important member of the underground (The Resistance) during the war. Through him, I did meet quite a few "resistant workers" and I became one of them.

He operated out of Rotterdam and I operated out of Amsterdam. I could depend on his help when I needed it. My main work was helping Jewish friends and relatives. After the War, Jack was decorated with the highest honor offer by The Netherlands: <u>Nederlands Verzet Kruis</u> (Netherlands Resistance Cross). Sadly, Jack passed away in May, 2018.

I know nothing of my parent's courtship – only that they were married in Rotterdam in a civil ceremony in 1920. Gerzon, the special women's fashion retail shop, he worked for moved my father, shortly after their marriage to Amsterdam. They had a factory in Amsterdam. He was very artistic. He designed their clothes and eventually headed the factory before he became the general manager of their stores in Amsterdam.

Carla's parents at their wedding,
November 18, 1920 in Rotterdam, The Netherlands.

My Childhood

I remember a story my mother told me. When they moved, a box of their best china dropped down some steps, most of it broke. She sat down on the steps and cried. My father sat down next to her with a big towel and tried to cry as well. This made her laugh and he told her it could be replaced. My son, Marc, could or would do the same!

My father's name was Marcus Olman. His Jewish name was Mordecai; he was known his whole life as Mor or Morrie. He was born in Rotterdam on March 10, 1895. My mother's name was Johanna Antonia Maria Jansen. She was called Jo. She was born in Rotterdam on August 3, 1896.

I was born at home on November 7, 1923 in Amsterdam. My father had to register my birth at the city registry. My father was supposed to register me as Carolina, after my mother's mother. Apparently, he did not like this name. He also was disappointed that I was not a boy, so he registered me simply as Carla. My sister Miep (Wilhelmina) was born thirteen and a half months before me.

Carla's parents, Morrie and Jo Olman on the beach in Zandvoort, where they often spent time in the summer of 1935.

My father worked 25 years for Gerzon, the fashion house I described earlier. In 1936 he started his own business. It was called HODACO, which means Hollandse Dames Confectie (translated Dutch Ladies' Manufacturer). He partnered with Gerard and Annie Pieck, German Jews who had fled to Holland.

Carla's mother, Jo, and sister, Miep, and Carla as a baby 1923
We had a normal and happy childhood. My mother was a
housewife, a good cook, a hostess, etc.

Miep and Carla 1927-1928.

He designed and manufactured ladies' suits and coats and, later fur coats were added. In the beginning, he toured Holland to show and sell the clothes he had designed and manufactured, to many different boutique type retail stores. Later on, the different department stores, particularly Gerzon, became one of his largest clients; they and larger fashion retail outlets would come to him at the factory showroom to view and purchase the change of season styles.

Once a year, there was a fashion show from all the Dutch designers at a castle or a fine hotel in the country. I went along for a fashion show on one occasion when I was 12 during my vacation from school. There was a pool with waves, my suit tore and I couldn't get out of the pool until my father came with a towel. I went to the changing room where the naked models were changing into different outfits, much to my mortification.

Carla at school, her final year in 1940.

Education

I attended public elementary school not too far from our home. During the first three grades, my mother and our live-in maid would walk me to school and pick me up at noon. We went home for lunch and they walked me back to school at two where I stayed until four in the afternoon and I was picked up again. School was every day except for Sunday. Wednesday and Saturday were half days in the morning only.

At the beginning of first grade, I had problems with writing and arithmetic. I would add eight and five and my written answer of 13 was reversed and written as 31. I wanted to use my left hand to write, but wasn't allowed to.

I was forced to write with my right hand. I became very frustrated. My mother discussed with the teacher, Mevrouw Wijnands, about placing me in a special school. However, the teacher told my mother she could straighten me out. So my mother sent me to school with a red ribbon around my right wrist to remind me to use my right hand. And then, one incident caused me to be suspended from school for one day from the first grade. I was so frustrated learning to sew by following the teacher's instruction that I threw my sewing bag at her and walked out of the classroom.

Carla and Miep 1930-1931.

I liked school. I was always glad to go back after vacation. In second or third grade I had singing lessons and sang so off-key the teacher told me I could read a book instead. I was a good student and tried to please the teachers.

I liked math the best. The language lessons were not my favorite. This was apparent, when years later I sent letters to Paul's parents and his father would correct the letters. I was not very happy about this.

In fourth grade, I was already studying French twice a week after regular school hours. In High School, I had to study German, French and English. My English teacher told me to marry a man with a short name because of the way I wrote and signed my name.

I had trouble with Chemistry because the teacher was not a very good instructor. I was suspended from High School, also for a day. I don't recollect the incident exactly, but the teacher was a nazie. We went to his house, rang the doorbell and shouted something at him.

The Germans invaded Holland on May 10, 1940. The following week we had to do our "final written exams." The oral part of the exams was postponed several weeks, but I remember bombs coming down while I was doing those exams.

I intended to study for a medical technology degree. Initially, I briefly attended the University of Amsterdam, but changed over to a private college, The Medical Analyst (Technology) School of Dr. Steensma. Also, being a private school, the students were not required to sign a loyalty oath to the nazie government and there was no restriction for Jewish students. I enjoyed the studies, but by this time, I had gotten involved with the underground army and I had very little time to study.

Carla dressed up for one of the parties at Poseidon.

Poseidon Sailing and Rowing Club

This story would not be complete without telling how important the Sailing and Rowing Club was to my life at that time.

Before the war and even now, there were rowing clubs along the Amstel River in Amsterdam. The clubs had special membership requirements. The membership at Poseidon Sailing and Rowing Club was 95 percent Jewish. There were other clubs whose membership were mainly Protestant and other rowing clubs for Catholic students.

At the Poseidon Club one had to be 15 years old to join. One also had to be approved. I was anxious to row and lied about my age and was accepted at age 14. I started instruction immediately and often rowed at 7 a.m. before school started. I also rowed during free school times like Wednesday and Saturday afternoons. Miep joined as well, but she was more interested in the parties.

It was here, at the Club, we met the Markus brothers, Doris, Jules and Robert. We also met John and Jetty Pais and many others. Doris later on married Jetty; Jules married Jopie, my second cousin. John married Zus, Jopie's sister. John Pais had been my boyfriend before and early in the war, however, the Pais family had fled to the U.S. to escape the nazies in 1942. Robert Markus wanted to marry me after the war once the Pais family had left.

Carla is the third rower. The crew is wearing the official rowing uniform as this was an official race on the Amstel River.

Carla and friends wearing their regular training attire.
Carla is second from the left.

At the Poseidon Club, we experienced the first encounter with the "SS" and Gestapo (Geheime Stats Polizei). One afternoon in February 1941, they came in and arrested whomever they found of the Jewish boys who were milling around. I was not there when it happened, but I remember two of them very well. One was Hans Philips and the other one was Nico Roos. Both of their parents were close friends of my parents.

They were probably the first Jewish casualties in Amsterdam. At first we thought they were arrested by mistake and they would be set free. How wrong we were! That day 470 Jewish boys and men were rounded up in Amsterdam and only two survived and returned after the war. It was the first *razia* (round up) in Amsterdam, sadly followed by many more.

Last Olman Family get together in the Hague in April 1941.

The War

Our life was good until the Germans invaded Holland in May 1940. Conducting business became more and more difficult. In 1941 to 1942, all Jewish owned enterprises were confiscated. My father had officially "sold" the business to my mother's brother, Anton, and his wife, as they were not Jewish. They had to move from the factory on the Keizersgracht to the top floor of an apartment building on the Frederik Hendrik Kade. As it turned out, Anton started to cheat by stealing and selling bit by bit the beautiful material my father had salvaged from the Keizersgracht. He also started to sell some of the sewing machines and other equipment. There was nothing my father could do because

Anton was the official owner and we couldn't go to the police. So slowly but surely we lost everything. There was very little income. My mother had hoarded pounds and pounds of dried beans and quite a bit of chocolate. All food was rationed. Towards the end of the war; they allowed half a loaf of bread a week. There were no eggs, no meat, no milk, no butter, etc. We could buy sugar beets. It took hours to cook these because there was little or no power. The same was true for the beans. They kept us alive though!

We were hungry, but I do not remember that we ever complained about that. My grandfather, Meyer Olman, died in the spring of 1945. He literally starved to death. The food they had, he gave to his daughters who were the same age as Miep and me. He lived in The Hague. The Amsterdam police informed my father of his death. They had received notification from the police in The Hague.

I had a working bicycle and I had also stolen a German nurse's ID. I rode the bike to The Hague after donning a nurse's uniform which I had bought. I attended his funeral; I was the only family member present of his family including his children (nine in total) and grandchildren (12 in total). I went back and forth the same day. I was stopped twice by a German patrol. I was able to talk the authorities out of confiscating my bike and being arrested. No one was allowed to leave the city without a permit. That was Good Friday in 1945. A month later we were liberated.

I used the bike for most of my transportation. It was the safest mode of transportation for me because I was able to avoid roadblocks and other unsafe situations and I could make a quick getaway. Eventually, I needed new tires for the bicycle, which was almost impossible to purchase. The underground raided a sugar factory near Amsterdam. I was given some sugar, which I used to barter for new tires, and the remainder I gave to the people in hiding, whom I was responsible for.

The nazies confiscated my father's bank accounts and car. Our radio had to be turned in. Those who had two radios would illegally keep one so they could listen to the BBC. This was often done in a closet where we covered our heads and the radio with a cloth so no one else could hear that we were listening. Later on it was said that the most important daily announcement was the first sentence, "This is the BBC London." This meant that England was still free and that the Germans had not managed to conquer it.

The underground listened to the broadcasts and would put out a one-page bulletin with condensed news. Many a time I helped to make copies on a hand operated copy machine (a mimeograph machine). We would carefully distribute these copies. People were eager to read them, though it was very dangerous to distribute the copies.

The Germans required all Jews to be registered. This had never taken place in Holland before because it was an open society. Thanks to the fact that my mother was not Jewish, Miep and I were considered to be "Bastards" but we did not have to wear a Star of David. At first, in 1941 when we had to sign up for ID cards I had written down Jewish as a religion. So the ID card, I received had a "J" on it. My father was terribly upset, and rightly so. As the war unfolded and all the atrocities committed against the Jews became a fact of daily life, my father engaged an attorney who managed to get me a new ID card without the dreaded "J" on it. It took one year and lots of money to obtain this new card. This new ID allowed me the freedom to move around freely and gave me the ability to become involved in the underground.

Carla (second from left) wearing her Star of David before her ID was changed.

My first contact with the underground was through neighbors. I trusted them and I needed help to find hiding places for family and friends. Of course, more hiding places were needed. People who were going into hiding needed new ID cards, rationing cards, etc. I was furnished with a small machine to make fingerprints, also new fraudulent ID cards, which were printed in England and secretly airdropped over Holland. Sometimes a group of underground workers would raid a rationing cards office and those cards were distributed to us so we could use them for the people in hiding.

The way it all worked was amazing. To a small extent it became routine. However, it was very dangerous, one misstep and people would lose their lives.

I believe my parents, to a certain extent, were aware of what I was doing. We never talked about it though, because the danger was too high and they certainly would have tried to stop me.

I read the book "The Darling" by Russell Banks, the story of a girl-woman who was a member of the Weathermen, a group of people in the U.S. who were vehemently opposed to the government's policy of the war in Vietnam. They did everything to disrupt normal life. They were homebred terrorists. This girl describes all the illegal things she did. In her mind this was all justified for the "Cause." The Cause was to overthrow the government by sabotage and other things.

The book reminded me very much of what we did to disrupt the German war effort. Because we were an occupied people, the underground effort to fight the Germans was the opposite of terrorism. The means were the same, though and the German Occupiers looked at our efforts as terrorist acts.

My role was mainly to help those families and friends who were in hiding. I described some of those things earlier. I was young enough and unmarried and did not have children; thus the danger was only to me. I chose to ignore the danger I put my parents in. I was lucky enough not to get caught, though several times I almost was, like

47

when there was an inspection on the train I was riding in with the fingerprinting and ID making equipment in the bag next to me. On another occasion, two nazie officers came to the house to interview me. (They may have heard about my activities). I spoke fluent German at the time. I answered all their questions satisfactorily and they found no need to arrest me. It probably helped that I flirted with them and they flirted back. I believe, I was lucky because of my age. The soldiers preferred to flirt with me rather than confront me.

As we all departed the house after my interrogation, the officers offered to carry my bag with all the illegal equipment. If they had looked into this bag or it had accidentally opened, I would have been dead and not writing this memoir.

In the Underground, my primary job was to find a hiding place for Jewish relatives and friends. I then changed names and identification cards. I took them to their hiding place, where I would visit them routinely to bring food, medicine and/or ration cards so that their host families could purchase food. Sometimes they were ill or needed a dentist, or needed to exchange money, or sell a diamond or so. I was involved and did as much as I could, as well as I could. It was not always successful, but everyone I helped in hiding came out alive, even though one family was deported to a camp in Germany because their neighbors betrayed them. The nazie government paid 125 guilders for each Jew reported and arrested.

A family I had known since the first grade sued me after the war. Before the war, The Netherlands had 1000 guilder notes. The Germans decided to eliminate the 1000 guilder notes. People would exchange these notes to smaller denominations at the bank. The family asked me to exchange 15,000 guilders; however, I was only able to get 50% of the amount because I went through the Underground. The family sued me after the war for the remaining amount of the money. Obviously, they were unsuccessful.

I guess, because I was young, some relatives and friends who knew me thought others could do a better job helping them. Those war years were horrible, but at the same time, I was young enough, and daring enough, and to a large extent, it was exciting to fool the Germans. It was my way of fighting the war. I did my utmost to help save people's lives. I have always been and still am a charismatic person, who feels the need to help people, who really cares and who feels bad about being selfish. Many people do not understand this. Sometimes I wish I were different. It would have made my life easier. I would not be so driven by my conscience. I wonder if it is because of the proverbial "Jewish mother's guilt syndrome." The fact that I am so privileged and others are not. All of this sounds rather conceited though.

My biggest regret was that Tante Eef and family refused my help (they knew someone who would help them!). None survived. And, I only could save one of the five children of Tante Alie's children, Loutje. The nazies had already deported Tante Alie's husband. She was left in Rotterdam with the five kids and no money. I received a phone call from her neighbors that they were being sent to

Westerbork (the transfer camp for Jewish people in The Netherlands). I dressed up in the nurse's uniform and met the train in Amsterdam. I was able to take the youngest, Loutje, off the train. Nazie soldiers stopped me and I said he was ill and had to take him to the hospital. During the war, he was moved from family to family. After the war, my parents took care of him and tried to adopt him, which was not possible because the Dutch Government took the responsibility for all the war orphans. He married and had a hard time coping with life. My father helped him. Sadly, he committed suicide in his forties. His daughter is still living today.

My life was a bit like "Miep" in Anne Frank's life story. The big difference being that the Germans called people like me "Bastards," which was a precarious spot to be in. "Bastards" were descendants of mixed parents (Jewish and non-Jewish). This made life dangerous for us, as we never knew what would happen.

We lived only a half a block away from where Anne Frank lived before she and her family went into hiding. We lived at 51 Noorder Amstellaan. After the war it was renamed Churchill-Laan. Anne Frank lived on the Merwede Plein. I often played in the small square on the Merwede Plein. At the time the east end of the square had the only "wolkenkrabber," (skyscraper) in the city. While Anne was five years younger than I, her sister was closer to my age. They attended the same synagogue, the reform congregation with Rabbi Mehler. In 1939, Anne and her sister, Margot and I all performed in the Purim play.

There are many details of those years I cannot remember. We had five years of occupation. The first six months were not bad. Gradually, the nazies tightened their grip and life became more difficult month by month. There was not sufficient food or heat. At the end of the war there was no power. We had carbide lanterns. The only thing one could buy was sugar beets. There was no gas or electricity to cook with. We used an old coffee can, put wires on the top and bottom and took charcoal from between the railroad tracks to heat the can which we put on a coal stove. It would take hours to cook the sugar beets with this method. It was an immense relief when it was all over.

In August of 1944, the southern part of Holland was liberated, but the northern part, everything north of the River Maas, which included the cities of Amsterdam, Rotterdam, and The Hague, had to suffer through a record cold until the spring of 1945. Twenty five thousand people died from hunger, disease, malnutrition, cold, etc. We, my parents, sister and myself made it through the war. Very, very gradually life became livable again.

Carla, as a medical officer (Second Lieutenant) in Amersfoort Camp where Dutch nazies were interned in 1946.

Life After The War and Romance

Shortly after the war I was hired as a medical officer by the Dutch Government Internment Division. In The Netherlands the government had taken over all the nazie camps. In Kamp Amersfoort they interned the Dutch nazie men. I was in charge of the lab and pharmacy. The food was pretty atrocious and many prisoners requested a special diet. I decided before allowing this to test to see if they really needed it. I ordered their stomachs to be emptied and the contents tested, using no anesthesia and placing a tube directly into their stomachs. Most requests were withdrawn after this. Sweet revenge!

I left after half a year and joined the Blood Transfusion Service of the Royal Dutch Army Nurses Corp. I was made a 2nd Lieutenant. I never needed to go to boot camp. I lived at home and was reimbursed for living expenses.

Thanks to the Marshall plan, my father was offered loans by different banks to start over again. He returned to manufacturing women's coats, suits, etc. The factory was named "Olman Dames Confectie en Bont" (translated as Olman Women Manufacturer and Furs). His product label was "Royal Coat." Fortunately, he became successful again. Initially, he rented a very large house on the Frederiks Plein. It was a beautiful five-story building. The upstairs two stories were used for the business. We lived on the three lower floors. The house was beautiful inside, with lots of marble and very fine woodwork and cabinets. The house had a dumb waiter from the kitchen to the dining room. We often put the dog in the dumb waiter. The heating unit was old. So were the pipes. One cold winter the pipes broke and the marble entrance turned into an ice skating rink and the front door froze shut. It took several years after the war until parts were again available to repair a leak or broken-down equipment.

My sister Miep married Dave Philips in February 1947. We still lived in the house on Frederiks Plein. Paul and I got engaged there. I had met him at the University Library in downtown Amsterdam on the Singel. Paul had rented a room in a house on the Amstel River. He did some research at the Tropical Institute and at the University Library. He was writing a paper on cocoa. His intention was to go to Suriname. I went to the library to study for the entrance exams to medical school. I had finished my medical technology degree and was working towards a physician's degree. I had made the decision to become a medical doctor. I really was not interested in getting married in the near future.

Carla and Paul romancing in 1946.

As it was, Paul noticed me (I did not notice him). He followed me a few times when I left the building. Finally, he asked me to join him for a cup of coffee in a café, on the corner of Singel and Spui in Amsterdam, which is still there. We talked and talked. The next time the same thing happened. My birthday was coming up, so I invited him to my party. It was the first big party after the war on November 9, 1946. He did not know a soul. The power was off and we had to light the house with candles.

Paul in 1946.

He and I ended up sitting on the staircase (which was grandiose) and he asked me to marry him. I said yes with some hesitation, because he was younger than me by one year. A few days later he donned his tail coat suit, bought a large bouquet of roses, rang the door bell (I was not home) and asked my parents for my hand. My mother was very impressed by all of this. Our official engagement reception was March 16, 1947. This included a large reception still in the same house on Frederiks Plein.

My parents moved that spring to a re-built house on the Memlingstraat. The house was one of the few houses bombed out by the allies, because across the street was a school building which was taken over by the nazie waffen SS. The building housed all the records of the Jews of Amsterdam, which were destroyed. Unfortunately, it was too late, because most of the Jewish people had been deported by that time. By having the records destroyed, the nazies did not have much information to proceed with. This helped those of us who were still around.

Paul and Carla on a Sunday afternoon on the Amstel River in a wherry boat (the boat's name was Wilca, a derivative for Wilhelmina and Carla) in 1947.

Paul and I married from the house on Memlingstraat. We had first been married in a civil ceremony on November 12, 1947 at City Hall. On the 15th of November, we were married again in the Church at Jacob Obrechtstraat. A reception and dinner followed in the Muziek Lyceum.

Our wedding on November 15, 1947 in Amsterdam.

*My dress was made by my sister in my father's factory.
Following the wedding many other women wore this dress at
their weddings.*

Paul had just finished his Dutch agricultural engineering degree at Wageningen University. He had started at the University when he was 16 years old. However, the University was closed in 1942 after all the students refused to sign a loyalty declaration to the nazie government. He returned to the University in 1945 and finished in two years. He was 23 years old.

In the intervening war years Paul had to go into hiding. At first he worked on a farm. Farmers were needed and were exempt from working in Germany in the war factories. He was twice arrested to be sent to Germany. The first time he induced his own asthma attack and was disqualified. He did this by smoking cigarettes laced with sugar. The next time he was being interviewed by a nazie officer who was called away for a phone call and a German soldier in the room opened the back door and let him flee.

He spent the rest of the war at his parent's home in hiding. He was not able to go outside. The one-time soldiers came looking for him, he hid himself in the attic, which was only accessible through a trap door in a closet. Luckily, the Germans never found the trap door.

The Peperzaks; Paul (sitting on left), Hannie (standing on left), Corrie, Greet (mother), Ad, Adri (father) and Koos back in Holland in 1933.

Paul's Childhood

A few words about my husband Paul. He was born in Djati Nigara, a suburb of Jakarta, which was named Batavia, Nederlands Oost Indie.

Indonesia was called Nederlands Oost Indie because the Dutch colonized the country for over 300 years. It became independent from Holland in 1945 and acquired the name Indonesia in 1948.

Paul was the fourth child of Adri (Adriaan born June 4, 1888) and Greet (Margaretha Catharina Teppema born August 19, 1891) Peperzak Teppema. They were married in

Holland in September 18, 1913. Shortly after their wedding they moved to Indonesia.

His older siblings were Koos (he became a Franciscan priest), Corrie and Hannie. Ad was his younger brother by five years. Paul and Ad were close friends all of their lives.

Greet and Adri's engagement photo in 1911.

Paul's parents moved to Indonesia in 1913, because his father had accepted a teaching position from the Government. He taught Dutch, The Netherland's language.

Paul was born on October 26, 1924. Shortly after his birth, Paul became ill with an intestinal obstruction. He was hospitalized for over three months. Fortunately, he was eventually cured.

In 1932, the family returned to The Netherlands because Koos, the oldest son, was ready to go to the University.

Paul was eight years old. He was old enough to remember his life in Indonesia with fondness and nostalgia. He always wanted to go back and live there again. And because of that he chose to study Tropical Agriculture. His dream was to manage a plantation.

Ad and Paul with their mother,
Greet, in Malang, Indonesia in 1932.

Because of wars, politics and citizenship that dream was impossible to fulfill. He was always a good student. He spoke many languages fluently and he could read many more. His father made him read the Canterbury Tales in Old Dutch when he was young. Old Dutch is closely related to Old English. The result was that at an early age he learned to understand both languages. He was very active in scouting and attended the World Jamboree in Holland in 1937.

Paul wearing his Boy Scout pin after having attended the Boy Scout World Jamboree in The Netherlands 1937.

He was always asthmatic which kept him from participating in many sports. However, he was quite artistic and very musical. He played the piano for hours – mainly classical music. He also liked to draw and paint and to write. Gardening was his life.

Paul had a great sense of humor, he was suave and debonair and very well dressed. He always wanted to own a convertible, but I discouraged him because of his lungs and the amount of dust associated with convertibles. He was a real gentleman, as it says in his obituary from 2001 "Paul was a gentleman's gentleman."

Paul headed to the U.S.A. on the SS Noordaam
December 13, 1947.

Voyage to America

In 1947, during his last year at Wageningen University's agricultural program, Paul applied for a scholarship in the U.S. through the Institute of International Education. Only two scholarships to his university were awarded that year. He was one of the two lucky ones. It was suggested he should attend Iowa State College in Ames, Iowa. We had no idea where that was! I was asked several times, "Aren't you afraid of the Indians?"

Paul asked to go to Florida because he thought that the university there would be more geared to Tropical Agriculture. His degree was in that field. At the time there were only two or three universities in the States which had top agriculture schools: Cornell in Ithaca, New York; Iowa State University in Ames, Iowa and University of California in Davis, California. Before he knew that he would get the scholarship, he was tempted to join my father in his business.

My father, having no sons, was looking for an heir to the business. Dave, my sister's husband, was not the right person. He was more of a salesman, not a manager or a people person. He also lacked the creativity to design clothes. Paul liked the idea. However, when he told this to his father, his father told him to finish his university education and to make up his mind later. Of course, taking over my father's business never happened.

We had decided to get married before he went to the States, so it would be easier for me to follow him. We married on November 15, 1947 and he left for the U.S. on December 13, 1947. I was very lonely even though I lived at home with my parents. I had no idea when I would be able to join him. As it turned out it was not all that long because in February 1948, I left Holland.

Leaving Holland was not easy in those years. The Dutch government required permits and, of course, the American government required a visa. Paul had entered the U.S. on a student visa. All I could get was a visitor's visa, which was only good for 6 months and could be extended for 3 more months. When I applied for the visa at the American Consulate in Amsterdam I had to prove that we had no intention to stay in the U.S. How do you prove that? I had just received a letter from Paul with an article about an interview he had given to the student newspaper. During the interview, he was asked what his future plans were. He told them that he was studying tropical agriculture so he could go back to Indonesia. My consulate interviewer accepted that.

If I remember correctly, the crossing to the U.S. lasted eight days. I had first class accommodations on the SS Westerdam from Rotterdam. It was a very nice cabin, which was a blessing because I spent a lot of time in it. I was terribly seasick! Upon Paul's departure for the U.S. on the 13th of December 1947, I met a woman. We were both waving goodbye to our men. Her husband was leaving to work for The Netherlands' embassy in Canada. Then lo and behold three months later on the 8th of February 1948, we were on the same ship, when I was finally able to depart for the U.S. She was so very helpful and brought me food and medicine while I was sick in the cabin. We exchanged Christmas cards for a number of years but lost track of each other several years later.

Upon my arrival in Hoboken, NJ, a girlfriend from Holland met me. I did have difficulties understanding the American language. I knew English pretty well as I had had 4 years of English in high school. My first impressions were wonderful. Before leaving Holland I had been asked by a medical researcher who worked on the Rh-factor to take a vial of frozen blood with me, which had to be delivered to a lab in Houston. The blood had to be kept frozen and was stored in the freezer on the ship. Upon arrival, at first, I was at a loss on how to get the vial to Houston, Texas as fast as possible, but then figured out a means by which to do so.

Paul and Carla's visa photos for the U.S.A. Carla is wearing her 2nd Lieutenant Uniform. September 1947 and January 1948, respectively.

When my friend drove me to New York, I noticed Red Cross flags everywhere. It was "Red Cross Week." It gave me an idea. I asked her to drive me to the Red Cross Headquarters in New York. Once I arrived, I explained my problem. They proceeded to give me a car and driver who took me to La Guardia airport. We met with the pilot who was flying to Houston that day. I personally handed over the vial to him. He promised to deliver it A.S.A.P. to the right place. This only can happen in America. I never heard if the vial was delivered.

The next remarkable and well-remembered event from my first 24 hours in the States was on the train to Des Moines, Iowa. I do not remember how many hours I was on the train, but I slept two or three nights on the train. For my first meal in the dining car I ordered two sandwiches from the menu. The waiter looked at me, shook his head and said that one would be plenty. I had no idea how sandwiches were served in restaurants in the U.S. In Holland, when you ordered a sandwich, it was a single slice of bread with a piece of cheese or meat. I tipped him, of course, but after awhile, when I was back in my cabin, the waiter came by and returned the tip to me. I never found out why he did that. However, it was a very nice gesture, which I appreciated because I had very little money.

Our arrival in New York in 1947 and 1948.

In the first years after the war the Dutch government did not allow any money to leave the country due to the dire financial situation in the country. All I was allowed to take was 25 dollars. I smuggled some more money by putting the dollar bills behind the pictures in the photograph albums from our wedding. Somehow the custom officers must have thought that I had diamonds or money hidden because upon departure from Rotterdam, before entering the ship, they took me aside. I had to undress and they examined every piece of clothing I was wearing. They did not find anything.

From New York I took a train to Des Moines, Iowa where Paul met me. It was great to see him again. When he left Holland a month after our wedding, I didn't know when I would see him next. It took him a good month once he arrived in Iowa to find someone to sponsor me for a visitor's visa.

*Carla arrived by train in Des Moines; Paul borrowed the
Studebaker to drive Carla to Ames, Iowa.*

Ames, Iowa

Paul had found a motherless family of three kids plus a
father, Mr. Smeltzer, who were looking for a couple to live
at his house and take care of everything; the children,
cooking, laundry, shopping, etc. It was quite a job. The kids
were good, but Mr. Smeltzer was a difficult man and it was
hard to keep things clean. I would have run away just like
his wife did, if I had been married to him! There was little
money for feeding the kids, the household and clothing, but
he spent a lot of money on film and photographic
equipment. He did sign my visa papers so I could get a

visa. After several months we found a basement apartment and we left that family. I found out I was pregnant.

The wife of the couple who owned the basement apartment was French. She was very kind to us. We had an icebox, which needed blocks of ice.

There was no air-conditioning, but we had a fan. We also had very little money to live on, but we never felt poor. I was in Ames from February to September 1948. Paul had arrived in December 1947. The Newman Club on campus had an international group of students. We took part in some their events.

Paul did a lot of soil testing in the lab. In Sioux City, Iowa, Paul's professor suggested that he take soil samples of a stored manure pile in a stockyard, which had been piling up for 50 years. He slipped into the manure and sank up to his chest, almost drowning before he was rescued by someone throwing him a board. He went to a rooming house and took a shower with all his clothes on. He attempted to dry his clothes between the mattress and metal springs, which left an imprint of the springs on his clothes. The trousers could stand up unaided the next morning. I later tried cologne, soaps, shampoos, etc. to remove the stench, but I was never successful! I could have helped him in the lab since I had a medical technology degree. However, the smells were pretty bad and being pregnant I got easily nauseated.

Before Paul completed his Masters degree in Soil Management, he applied to the Firestone Plantation Company in Akron, Ohio. He was flown there for an interview—his first airplane ride ever and it was a DC3.

Later on, of course, he logged over a million miles on airplanes travelling the world for business.

He was hired as a planter and was scheduled to leave for Liberia, West Africa as soon as he finished all the requirements for his Master's degree. Paul managed to do this within nine months; despite having to rewrite his thesis entirely. Professor Black felt the sentence structure was too much like Dutch and not in an American English style. Most Masters degrees take two years to complete so to do it in nine months was almost unheard of!

He missed his graduation ceremony, yet again, as we moved to Liberia. He had missed his graduation in Tropical Engineering from Wagenining University when he left The Netherlands for the U.S. I was supposed to pick up his diploma from Wageningen. His peers took bets on what I was going to wear to the graduation. Most of the students wore tail coats, I, on the other hand, was working and wore my dress uniform from the Royal Dutch Army. So they all lost their bets! He also later missed his PhD graduation in Iowa when we moved to Hawaii.

Normally, a planter is sent without his wife and family and they are allowed to join him six months later. We had no money and my visa was running out, so Paul requested that I be sent to Holland and that I pay my own way to Liberia. Firestone said this was unnecessary and allowed me to accompany him to Liberia. We were very happy about that. I was six months pregnant by this time. Much later, we learned that other planters were jealous that we had arrived together.

*Carla (pregnant with Marc) and Paul in New Orleans
waiting for the boat departure.*

Life in Liberia

We left Ames in September 1948 to go by train to New Orleans where we were to pick up the ship to take us to Monrovia, Liberia.

A few months before, we had gone to Chicago for shopping and sightseeing. We had to buy some much-needed items for the baby (Marc) who was on the way. We had very little money because the Dutch government still did not allow any money to be sent abroad. Paul's major professor, Bill Pierre, head of the Agronomy department of the university, loaned us $500, to be paid back however and whenever we could. We bought a bassinet, diapers (the ones that needed to be washed) and basic baby clothes at Marshall Fields in Chicago.

Paul on the ship, finally on the way to Liberia.

The stuff was sent to us. However, when we left Ames, we had to carry all our belongings to the ship with us. We had suitcases, several steamer trunks and the bassinet. When the train pulled into the station the compartment in which we had our seats was way back on the tracks and had not reached the platform. The train had to pull up so we could board. Everybody was nervous because the short stopping time was fast passing. The conductor tried to help us. Paul wanted to tell him to hurry up which is in Dutch "Schiet op." He told the conductor to "Shut up!" which did not help matters! Later, as we were all settled and the fellow came by, Paul apologized and tried to explain why he uttered those words!

We transferred in Chicago with the help of a couple of porters. Arriving in New Orleans, I can still vividly remember how shocked I was to see bathrooms for Whites only and for Blacks only!

The freighter, which was to take us to Liberia, West Africa, was delayed because they had to refurbish it from being a war troop transport to a passenger transport. There were only 12 staterooms. We had to spend more time in New Orleans, which was okay. Only, we were very short of money not realizing that Paul was on Firestone's payroll as soon as we left Ames. Also, the company was going to pay our expenses. There were no credit cards in those years! We were so young and inexperienced.

The crossing lasted over three weeks because one of the ship's engines broke down. I was seasick all that time. I stayed in our cabin for most of the trip. Paul was hired by Firestone Rubber Plantation in Liberia and on October 16, 1948 we arrived in Monrovia, the day Ellen, Miep's daughter, was born.

I remember vividly arriving in Dakar and my first impression of Africa and Africans. I was scared, but intrigued. Ever since that time I have had a certain nostalgic feeling about Africa. I loved the people in Africa. I found them proud, but kind, no chip on their shoulders. One can respect them and, in turn, you are respected. Almost 70 years ago that was the case! Also in Africa, in the interior, especially in the early morning, the land is quiet and beautiful. It evokes a certain atmosphere, which I cannot

74

describe adequately – peaceful and full of the promises that the land holds.

THIS IS ONE OF TWO PLANTATIONS WHICH HAVE 19,500,000 RUBBER TREES PLANTED ON 90,000 ACRES. 25,000 MEN ARE EMPLOYED TO PRODUCE 90,000,000 POUNDS OF CREPE RUBBER AND CONCENTRATED LATEX ANNUALLY. ON THESE PLANTATIONS THERE ARE:

YOU ARE ENTERING
THE HARBEL AREA OF THE
FIRESTONE RUBBER PLANTATIONS

10,000 HOUSES, A MODERN TELEPHONE SYSTEM, 2 HOSPITALS WITH A 3000 KILOWATT HYDRO-ELECTRIC 200 BEDS, POWER PLANT, 3 CLUB HOUSES, THE UNITED STATES LIBERIA RADIO 2 GOLF COURSES, STATION, CHURCHES AND SCHOOLS, A BRICK PLANT AND MODERN FACTORIES, 175 MILES OF ROADS. LABORATORIES AND SERVICE FACILITIES.

WE HOPE YOUR VISIT WILL PROVE BOTH INTERESTING AND ENJOYABLE

Carla and Paul arrived on October 16, 1948 in Liberia.

Monrovia did not have any pier, so we disembarked with luggage and all our belongings into a small boat, which took us to the shore. We were welcomed by a Firestone representative and taken to a beautiful company guesthouse.

A few days later we were driven to the plantation, about 40 miles or so on a bumpy road, full of potholes. This was the main road to Monrovia which led past Roberts Field, the airport. The U.S. Military actively used Roberts Field during the war because of its close connection and friendship with the Liberia, which means "liberty."

Liberia was settled by freed U.S. slaves. The capital Monrovia is named after President Monroe, who freed slaves and helped them return to Africa. The government of Liberia was based upon the form of government in the U.S. They even used the United States dollar.

For the first month we were quartered in a nice house we shared with a bachelor. It eased me into plantation life. There was no air-conditioning, so it was uncomfortably damp and sticky. We used fans. When our house on Division 23 was ready for us we moved there.

The house had a large living room, dining room and porch. It also had a fireplace! We used it once to smoke out a bees' nest, which had built up in the chimney. There was only one bedroom, a pantry and a kitchen with a wood stove. There was no electricity. We had a good-sized refrigerator, which ran on kerosene. In Liberia, the length of daylight only varies at most by about 30 minutes throughout the year. This is because Liberia is near the equator where the days and nights are approximately the same length of time. As soon as it got dark we lit many kerosene lamps even though we usually went to bed early.

Our water supply came from a small creek in the back of the house. Every day the barrel near the house was filled by carrying buckets of water from the dirty creek. The natives used the creek for washing, toileting, etc. We filtered the water and we took hand showers. For drinking and cooking, the water was boiled and filtered twice by Berkshire filters, which were huge.

Paul started out as a rubber planter. Rubber trees can only be tapped (milked) early in the morning from 6 a.m. to

10 a.m. Every morning, seven days a week, 365 days a year, the trees were tapped and every morning there was "mustering" and rubber tappers were hired. Only the foremen were more or less hired on a weekly basis.

The day started at 5 a.m. Paul learned after a while to put a pair of pants over his pajamas. He came home after the muster and slept another hour or so. The tappers got paid weekly. They only wanted hard cash, no paper money. So there were always heavy bags of silver dollars delivered to the division office.

Paul at work on the Plantation.

Paul was the planter of the division, the paymaster, the disciplinarian, the arbitrator, "the doctor", the marriage broker, the counselor, etc. They came to him with every problem. One of the problems he ran into was the conflict between the witch doctor and western medicine. When a tapper came to Paul, day or night, with a serious medical problem, injury, childbirth or whatever, and they insisted on being taken to the witch doctor, Paul refused and took the patient to the very well appointed Firestone hospital. Often the patient or the family refused to go there. Sometimes it was heart breaking to see the results of their insistence to see the witch doctor.

We lived almost five years in Liberia. That first house was located centrally in Paul's division. Our nearest neighbors were two miles away. There was no telephone; however, the "bush" communication was remarkable. If something happened within a short time, one of our servants would inform me. We never figured out how it worked.

I was not allowed to drive. If I needed to go somewhere, we would request a car and driver. Even visiting friends was done that way.

Marc was born on January 20, 1949, in the Firestone Hospital, and the doctor who delivered him, Dr. Qualls, was young, inexperienced and recently out of medical school. I was in labor for more than two days before Marc made his entrance. The hospital had electricity but there was no air-conditioning. In those years a new mother was kept in the hospital for two weeks. She was allowed to dangle her legs outside of the bed after one week. Marc was a beautiful baby, blue eyed, blond with perfect skin.

When we came home after two weeks, the steward was very impressed and if I did not hear the baby cry, the steward would come and tell me, "Missy, Master Boss cries!" It took some time to get "Master Boss" to be called Marc. When Marc was older he never played outside without a "small boy" attending to his needs. The reason was concern for snakes, killer ants and other creatures around.

We moved from the planter's division home to the "Research Area" when Paul was promoted and became a research scientist in rubber plants, diseases, soil, coffee, etc. In the "Research Area" where we lived, we finally had neighbors and a better water supply, though we never had running hot water. This also meant Marc's diapers were always boiled and were snow white.

There were five or six houses. The lab and offices and the Club were nearby. Life was very different. Most of the time there was electricity and the office had a radio and telephone. Our house had two bedrooms and was built high off the ground so less bugs, snakes, etc., could invade it.

We had a large lawn and garden. We grew our own oranges, bananas, papayas, avocados, pineapples and vegetables. It was wonderful. We imported some ducks. We fed them only fruit and since it was warm, they did not grow fat. They were the best ducks we ever ate. Also, they finally started to import frozen meat from New Zealand. Before that time, we only had canned meat.

The first time we could buy this frozen meat, we bought a lot and put about half of it in the freezer of Paul's boss', "Mac" McIndoe, who was on a three months home leave. As usual, the power would go on and off. One time the freezer did not kick back on. The result was disastrous! The smell! They never could get rid of it.

Our second home in Liberia on the Plantation.

Marian was born on November 14, 1951. We were on our second contract with Firestone. The doctor who delivered Marian was a German Count, Dr. Mogens Von Plessen. He was the "black sheep" in his family, because he studied medicine and for generations the family's only profession had been the diplomatic corp.

Years later in Thailand we became friends with Dr. Von Plessen's brother. Leopold Von Pleesen, who continued living in Thailand after he was forced to retired as a German diplomat. He was retired by the nazie government because he didn't agree with them. One of my memories of Leopold was that we always had exactly the same meal at

80

his house because his cook was only trained to make one meal for guests.

Dr. Mogens Von Plessen was good and very caring. During the last two weeks, before Marian's birth, he would visit me daily. Her birth was so much easier than Marc's. Again, we stayed two weeks in the hospital. Marc was delighted with his baby sister.

Carla having tea on the Palaver "talking" Terrace with Marian and Marc.

Marian was a beautiful baby. She had a lot of dark hair. She was sweet and good. Fortunately, I was able to nurse each baby even though Firestone would furnish baby bottles and formula if that was needed. By that time we had many friends and it became easier to raise the kids by comparing notes with other young mothers. Someone gave me Dr. Spock's book on raising children. He had many

81

hints in there especially about teething, tantrums and other minor childhood diseases. All this was very helpful since there were no parents or family to ask for advice.

Marc was about four weeks old when my mother came for a visit. This was a tremendous undertaking. It was February 1949; she flew on the largest existing airplane at the time. Like Paul's first airplane ride it was a DC3, which held 14 passengers. I believe it took two or three days; a night in Paris, a night in Dakar and on to Roberts Field in Liberia. Roberts Field was a good airport with a small terminal. Air France was the main airline serving flights from Europe. The airport was built during the war. American warplanes would fly to Brazil, the hump of South America, which is closest to West Africa. The Atlantic Ocean was crossed at this point being the shortest distance between the two continents.

For Mama, this was quite an adventure. Never before, nor after, did she undertake such a trip. She spent three weeks with us. We had only a one-bedroom house and poor Paul was sent to sleep in the living room. Of her visit there are two events, which I remember vividly.

I had a dressing table with a bath for Marc. She stood at one end and watched me bathing and changing the baby. All of a sudden, he peed, a beautiful long stream, which ended up perfectly in her décolleté. She was surprised to say the least.

Because of the lack of meat, we had our own live chickens and we would slaughter one for dinner. One day I told Mama that we were eating a chicken, which she had seen walking around in the morning. She could not eat it.

She had an affinity for chickens. When we were young, she had a pet chicken. The chicken would come into the kitchen to get a biscuit and milk. When we went for a month vacation to the coast at Zandvoort, the chicken would come along in a hatbox. One time the chicken had some leg problem and my mother put cotton around the injury to cure it.

Our life in Liberia was busy. I learned a lot about the American way of life; baby showers, parties and playing bridge. We did a lot of reading. There was no TV and most of our news came from listening to the radio. I read *Time* magazine, which was several weeks old, in detail from front to back. We sent long letters home and we received long letters back. I got an old sewing machine and learned how to sew.

Cooking was a challenge. We had to bake our own bread. We also roasted our own coffee beans, fresh from the plants. The kitchen was connected to the house via a pantry. This was necessary because we cooked on a wood stove. The temperature in the kitchen would easily reach 125 degrees Fahrenheit. We had a cook who could neither read nor write but he was very good at remembering what I told him. For the bread baking we had large 50 pound barrels of flour from the U.S. We had to sift the flour several times to remove most of the weevils that had taken up residence in the barrels. Paul had drawn pictures of the bread recipe with so many cups of flour, yeast, etc. It hung on the wall in the kitchen. We also had the cleanest diapers around, because they were boiled in stainless steel buckets called latex buckets, which were used, on the plantation to collect the rubber. The bucket stood always on the stove.

My first experience with baking a cake is worth writing down. Marc had his first birthday and every youngster (expatriate) of the plantation was invited to his party. I had no measuring cups and no measuring spoons, but I had an American cake recipe and also two pans. I used regular teacups as measuring cups, the same for spoons. Of course, it was a disaster. I made three cakes and put them on top of each other. The cake was not higher than two inches. A good friend, Betty Collins, rescued me. She baked the cake. She showed me all the stuff I needed and eventually I could buy them. We bought those things from people who left Liberia and went home for good. Most wrapping paper we recycled by ironing it. Betty also taught me about baby showers. We learned how to play bridge.

Paul worked hard and he spent months of his off hours on mapping a soil profile of the whole plantation. We found later that this was much appreciated because Firestone gave him a scholarship with no strings attached for as long as he needed it when he went back to Iowa State for his PhD degree. This was a complete surprise!

Living in Harbel surrounded mainly by American friends, we had decided to immigrate to the U.S. and to eventually to become American citizens. The U.S. consulate informed us that the quota for Dutch citizens was filled for over five years. However, when they realized that Paul was born in Indonesia and our kids in Liberia, they told us we could get our visas immediately. We were not ready to leave. When it was time, we got our visas under Indonesian and Liberian quota numbers! Interestingly enough, five years later in 1958 when we lived in Hawaii, which was not a state as yet, we ended up in a citizenship class, which was held in Japanese! How international can you get? Only in America!

We left Liberia by plane in 1953. It was Marian's first airplane ride. We stopped in Dakar, and flew in an Air France plane to Paris. It was a first class night flight with a small hammock for children. This hammock was tied to the ceiling and was above our seats. It was night and we all tried to sleep. Marian was 17 or 18 months old and in the hammock. All of a sudden I woke up and she was dangling head down with one foot (fortunately) caught in the hammock. She did not cry. I was furious with the stewardesses, who were asleep and never saw what happened. Fortunately, she was okay because she did not fall.

Maxie (the dog) with Jo and Mor.

Our Dogs

We always had a dog, however, once my father brought a "male" cat home. The problem was that a short time later the "male" cat had kittens. The cat and kittens did not stay.

When my parents first married they lived in Amsterdam and they had a German shepherd. He was well trained. He would bring my father the newspaper every morning.

The German shepherd could not stand cats. When Miep was born, my parents still had this dog. The dog would hear the baby cry, he thought it was a cat and he ran into the garden thinking there was a cat. He did not find anything. He ran back into the house and discovered the baby.

He immediately became her protector. She was in a bassinet and he slept under it. However, he was so protective that no one was allowed to touch the baby, except for my parents and the maid.

One day, my grandfather came to visit and the dog bit him on the legs because my grandfather tried to touch the baby. A year later, 13 months and 2 weeks to be precise (my mother always talked about the number), I came along and the dog became too much because he felt he had to protect both of us. My father tried to give him away, but the first try did not work. The dog walked seven kilometers back to our house. The next try was in someone's home that had a cat. When the dog went after the cat, the drapes with the screaming cat came down. I do not know where he ended up, but they did finally find a home for him, it was quite far away.

In Liberia, our first dog was a plantation dog, "Cokie." We were terribly fond of that dog. The people who managed the Coca Cola plant (hence the name "Cokie" on the Plantation) gave us the dog. When Marc was born, Marc became the center of our life and Cokie was just our "dog."

Over our married life we also had different dogs— some were problematic. In Hawaii, we had "Sputnik" who always ran off. Sputnik was named after the Russian satellite that had just been launched. The Sears store in Honolulu had a hot dog stand. Several times the store manager called to tell us that Sputnik was eating their hotdogs. Sputnik had to be put to sleep because he was impossible and he ran off all the time.

A friend of ours gave us another dog because we had children and the dog needed to be around children—so she thought. However, the dog was really nuts. She walked around in circles all day long. We had to put her to sleep as well.

In Rome, someone gave us a dog, a large one, who was so vicious. She ate the wood on the doors and completely ruined them. We returned the dog to its owner, who could not keep her and she was also put to sleep.

Thinking back, we had quite a few dogs that were difficult and impossible to keep. We, however, also had several good dogs.

Our last dog was Chaka. He was a wonderful mix between Dachshund and Hunt Terrier, born on our kitchen floor in Nairobi from Sheba. We got Sheba, a Hunt Terrier, as a puppy. We had tried to breed her with the same kind of dog but there was so much inbreeding in Kenya from that type of dog that it did not work. As it turned out, a three-legged Dachshund from the neighbors next door got to her. This was a very enterprising Canadian Dachshund!

Sheba stayed in Kenya with some friends when we left for the U.S. She was an older dog by the time we moved and an outdoor African dog would have had a difficult time adjusting to city living in a townhouse in Washington, D.C. Chaka on the other hand was just a puppy.

Chaka traveled with us from Kenya via Holland to Washington, D.C. to Colorado Springs. We took Chaka to Florida, to New Mexico to Kansas, etc. He lived to be 19 years old. His end was very sad. He could no longer see or hear. He was in the garage, Paul drove in, did not see him and he was hit by the car. His back was broken and he had to be put out of his misery. It was very sad. His ashes are now at my granddaughter, Lacey's house whose life he saved!

Sheba (Chaka's Mother) with Carla in Nairobi.

When we first moved to Colorado Springs, the house we rented had a pool. My daughter, Yvonne, and granddaughter, Lacey, were visiting. They were in the pool with Paul. Lacey in all of her three years decided to get out and to take her water wings off. I was sitting next to the pool; the telephone rang which I went to answer. Lacey walked back into the pool. Chaka (he did not like the pool and never entered it) noticed, he barked and jumped into the water. This got the attention of Paul and Yvonne and

Lacey was saved. The story was published in *Pet Smart* magazine in 1988.

Chaka with Sheba, his mother in Kenya, his birthplace.

Pammel Court 1955.

Ames, Iowa for Our Second Stay

We arrived in Ames, Iowa in August 1953 with two children, almost two and four years old. We lived in a duplex Quonset hut, next to the railroad. The first couple of weeks Marc would stand very excitedly on his chair whenever a train passed by!

The complex was called "Pammel Court." We lived at number 733. It was "temporary" student housing. It was demolished in 2004 - 51 years later! Because it was "temporary" there were no telephone lines in the units. Later on it was decided to install telephones. The units were very poorly insulated. Hot, hot in the Iowa summers and cold, cold in the winter. On the hot days we would buy a block of ice and put a fan behind it. This fan - ice combo cooled very well indeed.

Paul's Ph.D. was in soil management and statistics. His thesis subject was "How to manage and maintain the soil and slopes of Iowa highways" along with what to grow there. Many a week he traveled for four or five days to study the highway embankments and to bring back soil samples. He spent a lot of time in the lab researching the plants to grow along the highway so that they could decrease soil erosion. A few months before Joan was born he got ill. Strangely, his hands and arms were swollen. The doctor in Ames did not know what to make of it and sent him to the Mayo Clinic in Rochester, Minnesota. I went along, we went by bus. The neighbors took care of Marc and Marian. Marc stayed at the Halls and Marian stayed at the Munsons.

Paul spent five days as an outpatient over there. I went home after three days because of the children. They did every possible test and could not find anything wrong. The outcome was that he was allergic to the soils he was working with.

Joan was born the 8th of July 1954, on one of those hot and muggy Iowa days, in Mary Greeley hospital, as was Yvonne one year later on August 2, 1955. Joan was very light skinned and had hardly any hair. She was about 10 or 12 months old when she finally got her beautiful hair. She never cried, slept through the night, but the poor girl must have been hungry because she lost weight between her second and third month. Obviously, my milk did not have enough nutrition for her. She did well after being put on bottled milk. The problem was that I was so very busy with three kids. All my life I had had servants, I was not used to doing everything. After that, I never tried to nurse Yvonne. A wonderful advantage of this was that Paul, studying at night, would give them their bottle and I could sleep!

We lived in Ames for two and a half years. Marc attended kindergarten and first grade there. Marian entered kindergarten. She was the youngest in her class. The cutoff date for a youngster to be five years old was November 15th. Marian's birthday is November 14th. When we arrived in Ames, I tried to enroll Marc in the university nursery school. At first they said there was no more place for him. (Parents enrolled their children even before they were born). However, they did accept him because it was thought he was a good study subject because of his international background.

Marian was a good student; we did hesitate to send her to kindergarten because of her being so young. She managed very well until we got to Honolulu where she was in public school for six weeks and terribly unhappy. Fortunately, there was an opening for her at the Parish school where Marc attended and things got better.

Upon Paul's graduation from Iowa State University, he accepted a job with Dole Hawaiian Pineapple Company. In April 1956, the whole family moved to the Hawaiian island of Lanai.

Paul and Marc drove the car from Ames to Pasadena. I flew with the girls to Los Angeles. Marian was five, Joan was 21 months and Yvonne was eight months old. It was not easy. For Marian it was her third airplane ride, for Joan and Yvonne their first. Yvonne was so scared that she held tight around my neck the whole trip. When we arrived in L.A. there was no one to help me. I finally managed to get a taxi, which drove us to the hotel in Pasadena where we waited for Paul and Marc to arrive. We wanted to go to Disneyland.

The Disneyland Hotel was recently opened. Yvonne, not quite a year old, got a hold of a box of matches and ate the tops off of all the matches. This was the first time a doctor was called to the hotel. The doctor told me not to worry. The whole family then drove north to San Francisco. On the way, Marian got ill in Ventura. We had to stay a day longer. When we arrived at a five star hotel in San Francisco it was cocktail hour. We really felt like immigrants; dirty diaper bags, toilet seat, four kids and two worn out parents. We went to our rooms and decided on room service. Two days later, we flew to Honolulu, spent the night at the Royal Hawaiian Hotel and then flew on to Lanai.

1956 Peperzaks in Lanaii Hawaii
Peperzak house

The Peperzak home in Lanai.

Hawaiian Islands: Lanai and Oahu

Dole Pineapple Company added a small house to expand the space of the existing house to accommodate our family of six. There were four bedrooms and two baths. A beautiful garden was maintained by the company. Paul decided to raise chickens. He took care of them, as I could not stand them. When Paul was not there and I had to feed them, they would bite me and fight among each other.

Paul was doing research on pineapple plants and different soils types. Pineapple plants surrounded the house. The Dole Company owned the island of Lanai at the time. No passenger ships were allowed. People were always flown in. Those who came had to have some business with the company. There was a guest house with six rooms. There was also a Quonset hut where movies were shown on the weekends. There was a grocery store, a small hospital, a school and of course, the lab and offices. We lived on "Snob Hill," so called because only the management staff lived there. We were with eleven other families. Everyone knew each other and the kids were known all over the whole island. There were a lot of pineapple pickers, drivers, etc. that lived in plantation houses, too. The main labor force was made up of Filipino workers, years before it was the Chinese who did all the labor.

On the beach in Lanai 1956.

The Chinese, being ambitious and studious, made sure their next generation was educated and moved up in life.

Very few native Hawaiians were there. On the weekends we often went to Lanai Beach. It was about three miles from our house, a gorgeous bay, well protected, clean and white. Usually, we knew everyone who was there. We had many picnics on the beach. The first few times Yvonne ate the sand. It went straight through her and ended up in her diaper. Obviously, it did not do any harm.

There was one market on the island and all of our food shopping was done there. If we needed something special it had to be flown in from Honolulu. There was a small hospital with two doctors on staff, an RN and several nurse assistants. There was one medical technologist who also did the x-rays. When the technologist was ill or on vacation, he would ask me to take over. I still had two little ones at home, so we had to juggle hours when I could work. One time Joan needed her blood drawn for some reason and I had to do it. I felt terribly guilty that I had to take her blood since she was such a trusting, dear and happy child.

In school the white kids were in the minority. Each class had only two or three of them. The result was that there was reverse discrimination. Marian had become asthmatic as the result of a misdiagnosis by a doctor in Ames. Lanai, which is located in the Pacific Ocean, had a good climate, with one major problem; every afternoon around 4 p.m. the clouds came rolling in bringing a dense and wet fog. The trees on the mountain collected an enormous amount of rainwater. Paul did some tests and found sufficient water supply in the trees to provide a town of several thousand people. Poor Marian would get an asthma attack when the fog was dense. Several times she ended up in the hospital in an oxygen tent. We decided we had to move for her.

Joan, Marian, Yvonne and Marc in Lanai Hawaii in 1957.

Dole fortunately understood, and Paul was given the job as director of statistics of the plant in Honolulu. He had a double major Ph.D. in agronomy and statistics. So we moved to Honolulu in 1958. We rented a rather large house on Kewalo Street. We always said the termites were holding hands together and held up the house. It was pretty badly damaged by the termites. After we moved out the house it was torn down.

Life was much more expensive in the city and for a while Paul sold the Encyclopedia Britannica. Yvonne still has an original set of the books. He hated that job. When the army was looking for a teacher in statistics, he applied and was accepted and taught several evening courses at Hickman Air Force Base. The extra bonus of that job was that we were allowed to use the army facility at Waikiki Beach "Fort de Russy." So, many a Sunday we spent at the beach, which was the choicest piece of all of Waikiki's beaches.

Living in Hawaii was wonderful, as far as the weather was concerned. At the same time, the cultural aspects were quite limited. At the time, the Honolulu Symphony performed in a high school auditorium. The acoustics were not the best, neither was the orchestra! Paul traveled once a year to the mainland to attend meetings. I was getting a bit of claustrophobia. The kids were in parochial schools, Sacred Heart Academy and Maryknoll. The class sizes were around 49 to 50 kids. The discipline was strict and they did learn.

Marc was taking swimming lessons from Duke Kahanamotu, the most famous swimming instructor on the West Coast. Many years later a stamp was printed in his honor. However, Marc really did not care for it. He also took tennis lessons, so did Marian, but the Duke did not want them to do both because he felt tennis shortened your muscles and for swimming you have to stretch them.

After about two years in Honolulu, Paul felt confined in his office. Statistics was okay, but agriculture and being outside was so much more important to him. He also decided that his interest really was to work in tropical countries. He wanted to go into international development work and was anxious to improve the agriculture in developing countries. His degree from Wageningen was in

Tropical Agriculture; his original intention was to go back to Indonesia. His deepest wish was to become a plantation manager.

After our naturalization ceremony
on Nov 13, 1958 in Honolulu.

However, when he finished his Ph.D. degrees, there was no way to go back to Indonesia. The country was fighting for its independence from The Netherlands and they were also quite unhappy with the U.S. because of trouble in New Guinea. Actually, we went to Hawaii because it was a bit closer to the tropical dream Paul had.

Paul applied to the Food and Agricultural Organization (F.A.O.) from the United Nations. Their headquarters are in Rome. He was accepted as an irrigation engineer and agronomist for their Far Eastern office in Bangkok, Thailand. Another major change for the family! The kids were young enough to look forward to another adventure. I am trying to remember my reaction. I was glad to leave Hawaii, but rather worried about living in Thailand.

In Honolulu, we were active in Scouts. Marc was in the Boy Scouts and Marian in the Girl Scouts. For two years, I was a den mother and a Girl Scout leader at the same time. Paul was also involved as a Boy Scout leader. We were active in the church and I was a member of the League of Women Voters. However, we never made any real close friends except for Bill and Violet Young and their family. They were Chinese and wonderfully kind people. Bill owned a real estate company and managed the house we had bought at the naval base in Barbers Point at the outskirts of Honolulu. We purchased the house in order to store our furniture while we were overseas. The house was rented out furnished, usually to naval officers and the home was well taken care of. We were not allowed to take furniture to Bangkok; only personal items, clothes, books, pots and pans, etc.

The house we rented in Thailand was also furnished. We did not want to store our furniture in a storage unit in Hawaii and we also did not want to sell our furniture so buying the house at Barber's Point was a good compromise.

Bill Young never wanted any money for the work he did and we always felt embarrassed by that. We finally sold the house against his advice. We should have listened to him. We bought the place for $17,900. If we had kept the house it would have been worth well over a million dollars today. We kept in contact with the Young family for many years until Bill died. They were an example of a Chinese family where all the offspring ultimately became doctors and lawyers. The oldest son became a doctor, a lawyer and a pharmacist.

Honolulu, Hawaii in 1958.

Path to Citizenship

We became United States Citizens in Honolulu on November 13, 1958. Hawaii, at that time, was still a territory of the U.S. and we were granted our citizenship. Hawaii became the 50th state in March 1959.

It was five years after we had entered the United States with our immigration visas. The law required that before citizenship is granted, one had to attend citizenship classes, followed by an exam. In 1956, the Walter McCarran Act allowed Orientals to become U.S. citizens. Prior to 1956 that was not possible. The Act also allowed persons over 65 years, who were not able to speak or write the English language, to become citizens.

There were many Japanese people living in Honolulu and surroundings who finally could become citizens. So one day Paul took the afternoon off and we went at 3 p.m. to citizenship class. We arrived and we found that the class was conducted in Japanese. After 10 minutes the instructor decided to accommodate us, and in rather broken English announced that he would teach in English! That lasted also 10 minutes and he went back again to Japanese. We left. We had followed the letter of the law. Afterwards we spoke with our friend, the Director of the INS in Hawaii, who gave us a book to study, "*Citizenship in Twelve Lessons.*" We studied it, made an appointment for the exam and passed.

During the ceremony of which there were approximately 75 people who were being granted their citizenship that day, the judge called on Paul to ask him why he wanted to become an American citizen. Paul's answer, if I remember correctly, was "We live in the U.S., we make a living here, we pay taxes, and we like it." The judge was satisfied. For me the most difficult part of the ceremony was that we were told to renounce allegiance to our previous country of citizenship, The Netherlands.

Joan and Yvonne were American citizens by birth in the U.S. Marc and Marian, who were born in Liberia as Dutch citizens, (they had to be of African Heritage to be Liberian citizens) were too young to do the exam and to be sworn in. So we had to apply after our ceremony for them and the papers were mailed to us. We were then free to travel outside the U.S. and Paul was ready for a change.

Bangkok, Thailand in 1960.

Hawaii to Bangkok

Paul was accepted to work for F.A.O. (Food Agriculture Organization of the United Nations). He was required to go to F.A.O. Headquarters in Rome to prepare for work in Bangkok. We flew from Honolulu on a Qantas jet plane. This was our first experience with a four-engine jet. There was plenty of room on the plane. I remember how impressed I was that a cup of coffee did not spill and stood so steady on the tray!

We traveled with the children to Holland first. We had not been there in six years as we did not want to jeopardize our legal immigration status (the green card) by leaving the

U.S. The relatives had never seen Joan or Yvonne. It was 1959. Joan was five and Yvonne was four years old. It was quite a reunion. It was wonderful to see our parents and siblings. After a few weeks, Paul had to go on to Rome. I joined him later. The children stayed in Holland.

Morrie and Jo Olman in the 1960s.

Marc spent this time in Groningen with the Arens family; he went to school there. Marian spent some time in Waalwijk with the Lenglets, and Joan and Yvonne went to nursery school in Amsterdam. They were with me in the Memlingstraat at my parent's home.

One day, on the way to school Yvonne was showing off how she could skip and fell flat on her face in front of the lot where they were building the Hilton Hotel on the Apollolaan and lost her front tooth—root and all. Everyone went to look for the tooth. The tooth was found but the dentist said it was too late to put the tooth back in the mouth. It took five years to grow back.

Greet and Adri Peperzak in the late 1950s.

While Paul was in Rome he found a temporary rental apartment from a colleague and I joined him for a few weeks. The kids stayed in Holland. When Paul was ready to continue to Bangkok, I returned to Amsterdam to prepare for the family to move to Thailand. After Paul found a house in Bangkok (also a temporary rental) the kids and I flew from Amsterdam to Bangkok.

In those years we flew DC3s or DC4s. The K.L.M. plane was a prop jet. They were slow and it took quite some time flying. I remember we had to spend the night in New Delhi,

India in a K.L.M. guesthouse and continued on the next day. It took two days to get to Bangkok from Amsterdam.

Joan, Yvonne and Marian with Paul at the Bangkok Airport.

Yvonne, Joan, Marian and Carla in the Buick in front of their house in Bangkok on Sukhumvit Road.

Bangkok, Thailand

When we arrived in Bangkok, I thought the weather was unbearably hot. As it turned out, I had a high fever, which I apparently had had for a few days; because the whole trip from Amsterdam I had felt pretty bad. So the first thing I did in Bangkok was see a doctor.

We hired a chauffeur. Driving was not easy; the traffic was on the other side of the road (they drove on the left side of the road, like the British). Parking was difficult and I was unfamiliar with the roads. The chauffeur was overweight and perspired a lot. I often had to wait for him when I was finished shopping or visiting. So I decided I could drive myself and we let him go. This went well. I had only two accidents. One was when a bus pulled unexpectedly out of a bus stop, right into the traffic lane where I was driving. Our kids were in the car and so were several of the Murnane kids. The right rear fender of the Buick was torn off. I ended up with the kids at the police station. I telephoned Jack Murnane and I was out of there in 20 minutes. At the time I thought that was thanks to the diplomatic immunity we all had. Later on, I realized it was more than that. Jack's influence was powerful. The Murnanes were friends and we had met in Bangkok and our friendship continued over the years. For a longtime we had no knowledge that Jack was with the C.I.A. Jack Murnane was a secretary at the U.S. Embassy, so we were told. Years later when we all lived in the Washington, D.C. area, we were invited to the C.I.A. It was a retirement party for one of the directors, Jack Murnane! This was the only time Paul and I were at the C.I.A. headquarters in McLean, Virginia.

Bangkok was a big city full of life. We found a nice good size house in a compound with six other houses. There was a small silk dyeing and weaving plant right next door to our house. A Chinese/Thai family, who lived in one of the houses, owned the whole compound. There were two other expatriate families, the manager of the Bata shoe factory and the manager of the Proctor and Gamble plant. When Marc's only fitting pair of real good leather shoes were stolen at school, the Bata man made a pair especially for Marc. He casted Marc's feet, made a custom last and then made the shoes.

110

We met some wonderful people who became longtime friends; the Murnanes and the Fishers are the ones I remember best. We often got together for Sunday Brunch. Paul's office was in Bangkok, but the work was in the field, all over Southeast Asia. Because of the political situation, he could not go to Indonesia, but India, Sri Lanka, Burma, North Thailand and Vietnam, etc., were all part of his territory. He went often to India. Every time he went there he came home sick. Koos, his brother, who was a missionary in Bandung on Java, came to visit for a while. Paul traveled a lot so we were often without him. Life was busy. I had four children in school, which kept European school hours (9-12 and 1-4), though the school year started in May. The problem with the hours was that it really was too hot in the afternoon to be in non-air-conditioned classrooms. Picking the kids up at the hottest time of the afternoon and having to fight the chaotic Bangkok traffic - many of the *samlors'* (three wheelers) taxi drivers were high on drugs. It definitely was a daily adventure and a challenge.

The kids were in a Catholic school, Holy Redeemer, which followed the British School system and were taught by French nuns. Joan is left-handed and her teacher (a nun) told me she wanted to change Joan so she would get used to writing with her right hand. I could not say no to the nun, so I told the nun she could try it for two weeks. Having experience a similar thing myself, as a child I was forced to write with my right hand and I was not happy with the decision to force Joan to change. I think the nun realized that Joan couldn't be changed because I never heard a word about it again. Today she writes with her left hand!

There was no Girl Scout troop the girls could join, so Ilonka Fischer and I started an international troop. We called them the "Blue Birds" and we wrote their pledge in such a way that Buddhists and Muslims could say it also. We followed the Girl Scout guidelines. Most girls could not afford to buy a uniform so we used the blue blouses of the school uniforms. The girls seemed to enjoy it.

We had our first burglary in Bangkok. Paul had returned that evening from a trip and had left his attaché case downstairs in the hall. We did not have a dog at the time. We also had no servants living in the house. Someone broke the lock and screen door and took the attaché case. It did have his watch, gold cuff links, some money, a parker pen set, a dictating machine and all his papers from the trip in it. They had poisoned the two dogs that lived next door. We found most of the papers and the case in the *klong* (canal) behind the house. We rescued many sheets of paper and hung them out to dry. So, not all was lost. Fortunately, they did not take anything else. Unfortunately, Yvonne heard them sawing a hole in the door and woke Joan to tell her. Then Joan was a nervous wreck for some time. We could not get her to sleep. We ended up giving her a bit of whiskey to relax her. It worked!

The house had no hot water and even the cold water was unreliable. At the time we lived in the outskirts of Bangkok, near road 83 of the Sukhumvit Road. After we lived there for a few months, the city was able to get the water system running and the showers became usable. The weather was hot enough, so cold water showers were okay. We had to boil and filter the water for drinking. For cooking we used permanganate tablets to wash lettuce, vegetables and fruit. Many products were not available. Several times I went with Paul to Hong Kong and did the shopping there. There was a reconstituted milk plant managed by Foremost in Bangkok. So milk and ice cream were available, though we made our own ice cream. Local fruits and vegetables and fish were abundant. I often went to the market and spoke enough Thai to bargain with the merchants for the correct price. I also made our own peanut butter.

The Peperzak home on Sukhumvit Road in Bangkok.

Only one bedroom in the house was air-conditioned. The other rooms had cross ventilation. The power was also unreliable, so more often than not, we did not use the air-conditioning. We used fans in every room.

The television broadcasts were only in late afternoon and in the evening. Most programs were in Thai, which was almost impossible for us to follow. We didn't watch television often because of the power situation. The only broadcast I really remember from that time was the election debates between Nixon and Kennedy. That year was the first time we could vote for the presidential candidates and we voted via absentee ballot. Our news came mainly from Time magazine.

Joan and Yvonne were so close in age they had each other as friends. Marian and Marc had friends from school. Visits went back and forth. Many weekends were spent with the Murnane family. The Murnanes had five kids; their ages were close to our kids' ages.

We also became good friends with John and Ilonka Fischer. John Fisher was an army officer assigned to the U.S. Forces in Thailand. Their oldest son became a good friend of Marc, and their oldest daughter was a friend of Marian, the younger girls were Joan's age, and they played together. We kept in contact with both the Murnanes and the Fishers for many years.

In Bangkok, I got dengue fever. We took our anti-malaria pills very faithfully every Sunday morning; however, apparently they were not effective against daytime mosquito bites. We also tried to protect against mosquitoes by putting mosquito coils under every chair as soon as dusk came. We also did a lot of spraying with DDT (Dichlorodiphenyltrichloroethane). We did the same in

Liberia and I often wondered if that was one of the reasons for Paul's recurrent lung problems and later on, my COPD (Chronic Obstructive Pulmonary Disease – Chronic Bronchitis). Dengue fever is said to be caused by the daytime mosquito. Anyhow, I was quite miserable – high fevers, joint pains, etc. The doctor wanted to hospitalize me, but I did not want the kids home with only the servants to supervise them. Paul was on a business trip. I stayed home and it took a long time to get over it. In fact, for about ten years I would get a horrific headache twice a year.

Paul requested a transfer to the headquarters of F.A.O. in Rome, which was granted, and so again the family packed up and moved this time to Italy.

Peperzak Family in Rome, Italy 1965.

Rome, Italy

It was Christmas of 1961 when we arrived in Rome after a short vacation in Israel. The school system did not quite correspond to the British school system. Marc went to Notre Dame; the girls to St. Francis, both schools followed the American Curriculum. Marc was behind in Algebra, they did not offer that in Bangkok and everyone was behind in American History. Before we left we ordered the books from the States and I "home schooled" them in both subjects. It worked fine and there were no problems with their new schools. Marc actually skipped a grade.

We left Bangkok on Christmas Day 1961. We flew to Beirut and on to Jerusalem for a few days of vacation. We had an enormous amount of luggage because we were allowed extra baggage. We had arranged that most of the baggage would be flown to Rome and put in storage there until our arrival.

In those years people did not fly on holidays. The six of us were the only passengers in First Class. Then Pan American Airlines decided not to stop in Rome because there were no passengers to disembark or embark. So here we were in Beirut with the entire luggage, which included several trunks, boxes, suitcases, movie projector, etc. It was impossible to load all of these articles onto the small plane, which was to take us to Jerusalem. It took Paul an hour to get Pan Am to agree to send the stuff to Rome separately. We thought we would never see it again, but lo and behold nothing was lost.

We rented an apartment in EUR. We did not live more than a year in Rome. Paul was persuaded by David Lillienthal into joining the Tennessee Valley Authority (T.V.A.) as a research scientist. He was not sure if he wanted to go back to being a scientist, but he wanted to try it.

Marc graduated from the 8th grade from Notre Dame School. I have forgotten his name but a well known Italian Cardinal, who could barely speak English, was the speaker.

*Enroute from Rome, Italy to Florence, Alabama
on the S.S. Statendam in 1962.*

Florence, Alabama

Immediately after Marc's 8th grade graduation in 1961, we departed from Rome. The children and I went to Holland while Paul went on to Florence, Alabama to start his work with the Tennessee Valley Authority (T.V.A.) and to find us a house to live in. He rented a place and we took the Holland America Line SS Statendam to New York. Paul picked us up with the luggage I wished to keep with us. We had to rent a small U-Haul, which turned out to be the wrong thing to do because the car broke down in a small town, Emporia, Virginia. We had just visited the Murnanes who lived near Williamsburg, Virginia. We had to stay three days in Emporia because the parts needed to repair the car had to be shipped from Richmond, Virginia. Fortunately, there was a pool at the hotel. I believe it was a Holiday Inn. There was absolutely nothing else to do in that town. It was August and very hot and sticky. It was the year of the "Bay of Pigs" in Cuba.

We did not find any house in Florence, Alabama we liked to buy so we decided to build a house. I do not remember when we moved into the new house. I believe it was by the end of that year.

Yvonne, Joan, Carla, Marian and Marc in front of our home on 1701 Tune Avenue, Florence, Alabama.

Marc went to 9th grade at the public high school in Florence and the girls went to a small parochial school, St. Joseph; Marian was in the 6th grade, Joan attended 3rd grade and Yvonne was in the 2nd grade. Yvonne had a very

119

young teacher who could not handle her students well; she especially had trouble with Yvonne. The teacher was in tears. Yvonne not!

Paul again traveled a lot. He was assigned to start a research project near Ocala, Florida. The government had a plot of land there, which was mined for phosphate during World War II. Weyerhaeuser, the lumber company, requested T.V.A. to do a research project about the growing of trees, what fertilizer to use, which kind of trees to grow, etc. Paul loved setting it up. However, after the whole thing was established and the waiting game began, he lost his enthusiasm for it. He felt anybody could do the follow up work.

He also decided that the scientific/research work was not what he really wanted to do for the rest of his career. He wanted to get back into international work, to work in developing countries to improve the agricultural economies.

This was the time that there were many articles in the papers and journals, which predicted that there was not sufficient food in the world to feed all the people. He strongly disagreed, he felt there was enough land to grow more than enough food, but it had to be properly developed, irrigated, fertilized and taken care of. He decided to rejoin F.A.O. They were happy to have him back, so in 1964 the family moved back to Rome, Italy. By this time our belongings included my father's piano.

And, today, the Piano at Julie's home
following an extensive, costly refurbishment.

Papa's Piano

Papa (my father) had a baby grand piano, a Thürmer, built in 1923, the year I was born.

The piano is now in the tender loving care of my granddaughter, Julie. Papa would be pleased. Julie is the only grandchild who has had the interest in continuing to play the piano. It is also good for this made-for-the-tropics piano to be in Snohomish, Washington; not only will it be played, but the climate is ideal. There is enough moisture and never the dryness of Colorado.

The Thürmer baby grand piano in Colorado Springs 2001.

In 1961, the piano was shipped from Amsterdam to Florence, Alabama. My father could no longer play it. He did not feel well enough because of his emphysema. Paul was anxious to get the piano.

When we moved back to Italy from Alabama in 1964, Papa was not concerned about us moving, but he was unhappy about the piano having to move again.

As it turned out, the piano was flown to Rome. This was not too bad, as it was better than being shipped by boat. From Rome, it was moved to El Macero, California in 1967.

We moved from California to Washington, D.C. in 1972, and from Washington, D.C. to Colorado in 1988. While in Washington, D.C., we moved to Kenya and we did not want to put the piano in storage. Joan and Yvonne were studying at Georgetown University; we decided to buy an apartment for the piano and the girls, in that order!

One of the many moves of the piano –
this one into the Potomac house.

The family: Joan, Marc, Carla, Marian,
Paul and Yvonne in front of their home
in Casal Palocco, Rome, Italy.

Rome In 1964

They flew our belongings to Rome including my father's
baby grand piano.

For the first time in their lives my children travelled
with only their father. I spent the time it took them to cross
the ocean with my mother in Holland because of her health
issues. My mother had had surgery for her stomach and
while in the hospital, she developed a lung embolism. So
when we all left Alabama to move to Italy, I flew to
Holland to spend ten days with her. Paul and the kids took
an Italian ship, the SS Leonardo da Vinci, to make the

Atlantic crossing. I understand it was rough. Marc was seasick, but the girls handled it well. Paul had decided to go second-class, because he felt that if you go to work to help poor people you should not travel First Class! Later on, this was definitely not the case at the World Bank.

Our car, an Oldsmobile 88, went with them on the same ship. So when they arrived in Livorno, they could drive themselves to Rome. I arrived from Amsterdam the same day. At first we lived for a month in an apartment/hotel, then we moved to the house in Casal Palocco.

The second time living in Rome was a bit easier because we knew what to expect. Marc attended the International School, Marian initially attended Saint Francis as did Joan and Yvonne, but after her 8th grade graduation, she attended Marymount International School. Rome was a wonderful place to live; however, it was difficult for the children.

We lived west of the city in Casal Palocco. The schools were in the northern part of town. At night or in the early morning, with light traffic one could drive to their schools in 20 minutes or so. However, it took much longer on the bus. We would pick them up and dropped them off at the bus stop which was in EUR about 20 minutes from our house. Then the bus took about an hour and a half each way because the traffic was so terrible. The kids did not mind. They had a good time on the bus. I, however, did mind. I felt their days were too long. They left the house at 7:30 a.m. and did not get back home until 5:00 or 5:30 p.m. I was always glad when the weekend came. We considered moving closer to their schools. However, it was much more convenient for Paul to live closer to his work. There were only 181 school days in the year, so we stayed in the house.

Most people lived in apartments; we had a real house with a garden. When we moved into the house it was new and it took some doing to get everything to work just right. The wiring in the kitchen was crossed. The drainpipe of the upstairs shower was not connected. There was no telephone. We finally were able to get a phone. As a matter of fact, our name and number are still in the Rome telephone book so many years later, nobody wants to alert the phone company of a change, because they will cut off the phone line and it may take months to reinstate it.

Koos, Paul's brother, a Franciscan monk and missionary to Indonesia, visited us during the time Marian had her 8th grade graduation from St. Francis. He attended the event and everyone, especially the nuns, felt honored to have him visit the school. Saint Francis School was a small school. The grades were kindergarten through the 8th grade. The classes had no more than five students each. The school was started at the convent of the Sisters of St. Francis. The sisters needed some outside income and this was their answer. There were some boarding students; they taught the girls table manners at the school-served lunch. When my father died, the girls boarded at the school/convent. I was very grateful for that because it left me worry-free to leave them. This was in October 1965.

The school also had the girls perform in several plays during the school year. We never needed to be concerned about costumes because the Italian, non-teaching nuns would sew all the costumes. All we had to do was show up in the audience. It was a great place for the girls. I'm not sure Yvonne agrees since she was sent to the principal's office quite often.

Joan, on the other hand, enjoyed the school, the small classes and never was in trouble. Since she was so tall she always played a boy's part in the plays. She was Bob Cratchit in the Christmas Carol and Prince Charming in Snow White. In the Christmas Carol, Joan had to carry a small boy on her shoulders. He always had wet pants from peeing in his pants.

When Marian graduated with about six other girls, one started to cry. Pretty soon all the girls were crying! It was rather funny.

Marian attended Marymount International School in the 9th grade. This was a much larger school than St. Francis and we were happy to be able to meet many of her friends' parents.

All the schools our children attended were international schools and had students from all over the world. They mostly followed the American School Curriculum, thus the majority of the students were American; however, there were Dutch, Italian, German and Russian children and children from many other countries. Since the schools were boarding schools, many students' parents lived in places other than Rome. Quite a few students were the children of "Aramco" employees. Aramco is a large Arab-American oil company in Saudi Arabia. The parents lived in Saudi Arabia and the children lived in Rome.

I still remember vividly a New Year's Ball we attended in Rome. It was quite a formal affair. I had the dress on which was made for me in Bangkok by the seamstress of the Queen. The occasion for which the dress was made was my presentation to the Queen of Thailand. The Queen and her companions wore very tight dresses. So this dress was also very tightly made. In Rome, at this occasion, I had a cold. I started to cough and literally busted out of my dress. We had to go home. How embarrassed I was!

Paul was only a few months at F.A.O. headquarters when he was asked to join the World Bank-F.A.O. Cooperative program. This was a brand new program for the World Bank in agricultural development. He was one of the first five officers.

For me, the problem was that he would travel in the field for three weeks or so, come home for a few days and then go to Washington, D.C. to write his reports for another three to six weeks. Marc was 15 years old; he really needed his father's supervision. He had a driver's permit from Alabama. The Italian police did not know the difference between a permit and a license. I let him drive the FIAT Multipla, a small Fiat which was designed to hold six persons, however, the engine was not big enough to really transport six people in it. Without my knowledge, he must have had lots of his friends in that car, because the car's engine always had problems. I also wondered where he went with the car. He was only allowed to drive from our house in Casal Palocco to the bus in EUR, a suburb of Rome. Ha! Ha! Later, I saw in Marc's yearbook that he was called "Marc, the Fiat People Packer!"

When we were ready to leave Rome and we tried to sell this car, a young New Zealand couple wanted to buy it to tour Italy with it. Paul did not want to sell it to them because he felt the car was unreliable. A colleague bought it instead. A year later when Paul visited Rome, he saw the buyer at a party. He still felt badly about the condition of the car and tried to avoid him. However, the fellow sought him out and told him how pleased he was with that wonderful car!

Marc attended Notre Dame initially and the International School later. He graduated in 1966. He was the valedictorian; however, he had not prepared his speech, so he did not do a very good job. The week before his graduation there were several events at his school. One of them was a senior dinner served by the juniors. The senior fellows wore Roman togas (sheets) and headbands made from leaves. After the festivities were over they decided to visit the Forum Romanum, the only problem was the Forum was closed. They visited it anyway by jumping over the walls. The police came, ready to arrest them, however, most of them had diplomatic immunity (including Marc), and so they had to let them go. Marc left for the States the Sunday after his graduation on Pan Am flight 111 at 11 a.m. On board he met Robert and Ethel Kennedy who were returning from a State visit to South Africa. Marc managed to have a conversation with Robert Kennedy. In his letter home he wrote that Robert Kennedy was very tired so Marc decided to let him sleep.

Marc was on his way to Florence, Alabama where he had a summer job with T.V.A. He was a guest at Vic and Anne Kilmer's home. The Kilmers had moved into our house at 1701 Tune Avenue when we left for Italy. This was the one home we owned that I really liked. They eventually built their own house and we sold the house after they left it.

In September, Marc went on to Lehigh University in Pennsylvania, originally to study engineering. This was on the advice of his high school counselor in Rome, Italy. He was very good in math. After six weeks in engineering, he realized he did not want to become an engineer and he switched to the business school. We were still living in Rome. Paul visited him every time he was in the States, but it was not easy to communicate, the main contact was through letters.

We moved back to the States at the end of 1966.

The office of Peperzak, Fuller and Associates in Davis, California.

Davis, California

Paul was talked into joining D&R (Development and Resources Corporation). This was David Lilienthal's company. David was appointed by President Truman to head the T.V.A., later he headed the Atomic Energy Commission. David knew Paul and wanted him to head the agricultural division of D&R. It was a wonderful opportunity and after a great deal of soul searching Paul accepted the job. I was happy to return to the States. We settled in El Macero, California, close to Sacramento where D&R had opened the West Coast office with the idea to be closer to the University of California in Davis. The plan was to hire consultants from the University. D&R's main business was the building of a dam in Iran. David Lilienthal knew the Shah of Iran well. Once the dam was built in Khuzistan, the land needed crops and irrigation. That is where Paul's expertise came in. Once again, there was a lot of traveling involved.

Yvonne, Marian, Joan and José Philips
in El Macero, California 1968.

Marian went to Davis Senior High School, Joan was in the 7th grade at Emerson Junior High School and Yvonne was in the 6th grade in elementary school. For the first time in their lives, Joan and Yvonne were in different schools. Yvonne was terribly unhappy; she had never been in a public school. The language, the attitude and the class size all frightened her and there was no Joan to help her. Fortunately, a spot for her in the parochial school opened up and she transferred there. She became a much happier girl.

Marc was still at Lehigh University in Bethlehem, Pennsylvania. He had purchased a small car without our knowledge. Thanksgiving 1967 he drove to the Kilmer's house in Alabama. He decided to return Thanksgiving night to Pennsylvania and fell asleep while driving on the Pennsylvania turnpike. He ended up in the hospital; the car a total loss, also there was damage to the divider on the Turnpike. We were not informed until a few days later, and by this time he was out of the hospital. We insisted that he come to the West Coast and go to a university closer to us. He applied to the University of California, Berkeley and was accepted. He started there in January 1968. This was during the Vietnam War. At first, in order to stay out of the military service, one had to be a full time student. A year or so later, the government instituted a lottery. He was lucky, his number was high and he was not called to serve.

Marian, in the meantime, started to feel a bit more at home in school. During her junior year, José, her cousin, Miep's daughter, came to stay with us from The Netherlands. She shared Marian's room and they became good friends. They did a lot of things together. Marian was a very good student. José had to learn American English and took easier classes than Marian. Marian and José are still best friends.

We lived in El Macero for almost five years. Paul became frustrated with the management of D&R's headquarters in New York. He had become director of agriculture and he saw the work very differently from David Lillienthal.

David had hired Jerry Levin, a young and very ambitious lawyer. Jerry ended up being the President of Time Warner Company and negotiated the deal with AOL and Ted Turner. He became one of the most powerful CEOs in the U.S.

While we lived in Davis, I had several medical problems; one of them a thyroidectomy. It took a while to get over that one.

We made some friends, but never really close ones in California. We saw a great deal of Zus and John Pais. Zus (aka Kathy) being my second cousin and sister of Jopie Markus, and I were very close as youngsters. John was my boyfriend immediately before and during the first year of the war. He and his family fled Holland in 1941 and lived in the States during the war years. John joined the "Princess Irene Brigade," which became part of the Canadian Armed forces and he returned to Holland as part of the liberation forces. He asked me to marry him. I liked him, but not enough to marry him. We also had grown apart so I declined his offer. He then married Zus who had returned with her family from Mauthausen, the concentration camp, where they had spent over 24 months interned. The family survived because both Zus and her brother Hans were born in Argentina and they claimed Argentinean citizenship, which gave them a small amount of preferential treatment or immunity from the nazies. As I said earlier, towards the end of the war, Zus and Hans and the whole family were rescued by the Russians when the tracks were bombed by the Allies and the death train they had been put on couldn't continue.

Paul and one of his colleagues, Bill Fuller, decided to form their own company. They resigned from D&R. They did take several other employees with them. The company was called PF&A (Peperzak, Fuller and Associates). They worked hard, they did get some consulting jobs and they had a Peace Corps job-training contract. However, this was not sufficient to pay all the staff. They arranged a partnership with Foremost Company, a milk producing organization headquartered in San Francisco.

I had become a real estate agent and had joined a firm but I did not do much for it. It was before we left Davis. Marc was in Berkeley where he had become an insurance agent while he was a student to make some money. He was doing very well selling insurance to his fellow students. He met his future wife, Cherie Ann Rheault, at that agency. When Paul started PF&A, Marc underwrote their business policy. Foremost's management was in disagreement about the arrangement with PF&A and after about one year decided to pull out. This was the end for PF&A and Bill and Paul went their separate ways. Bill Fuller left to start his own marina. Sadly, Bill drowned in an accident at his marina. Paul contacted his old World Bank friends and he was hired as an agriculturist in Washington, D.C. at the headquarters.

Paul left for Washington, D.C. in January 1, 1972. Marian was a student at the University of California, Davis. Joan was in her senior year and Yvonne was a junior at Davis Senior High School.

We waited until the end of the Fall semester. Joan had enough credits to graduate from Davis High School, so she did not need to attend High School in the D.C. area.

The two girls (Joan and Yvonne) and I drove to D.C. It was quite a trip; we took the Southern route because of the weather. It was the end of January 1972. We stopped in several places; one I remember well was Fort Worth. We ate in a restaurant where I ordered Rocky Mountain oysters! The waiter asked me if I knew what they were. I said, "Yes." Of course, I could not eat them.

We stopped in Alabama to visit with old friends. Paul met us there; we drove through Knoxville, Tennessee where we visited with the Olivers. John Oliver was Paul's boss at D&R and they had become good friends.

Carla, Marian, Joan and Yvonne in front of our home
on Gainsborough Road in Potomac, Maryland.

Washington, D.C.

I looked forward to living in the Washington, D.C. area. Davis, California was rather a cultural shock after living in Rome, Italy. I liked big city life. We spent a lot of time in San Francisco. We went to stage plays, the symphony and the opera, but it was 80 miles away. We also had relatives there, Zus and John Pais. We enjoyed getting together with them.

Paul had rented a house in Bethesda, Maryland on Hamilton Court with the idea that Yvonne would live in that district and could attend Walt Whitman High School. At the time, it was listed among the top 10 high schools in the U.S. As it turned out, we lived on the wrong side of the street. She had to go to Winston Churchill High School in Potomac. Because of that we looked to buy a house in Potomac. We found one under construction and bought it for $72,000! Later on after our return from Kenya, we spent almost as much on renovating the house. Now, it would sell for over a million dollars!

Paul liked his job with the World Bank very much. However, his dream to work in the "Tropics" was still there. He applied and he was selected to go to Nairobi. Paul and I moved there in April 1974.

Even though we were moving, we bought a small apartment on Cathedral Avenue in D.C. The idea first came to me because we did not want to put the piano in storage, then it hit me why not buy an apartment? The girls can live in it and the piano had a good home! Joan was attending the University of Maryland and transferred to Georgetown University. Marian had come home after her 1973 graduation from the University of California at Davis and was working at a collection agency. She hated the job and was dating a fellow California student, Tom. She decided to go back to California even though she and Tom had broken up. Marian met her future husband, Bob, there on the ski slopes in California. They were married June 5, 1976 in California.

Yvonne was at Georgetown University School of Nursing. The girls (Joan and Yvonne) had to share a bedroom at the condominium at 3901 Cathedral Avenue. Joan had met Pat Conner, her future husband. Apparently Pat spent a lot of time in the place. Pat and Joan got married on July 4th, 1976 (the American Bicentennial). Yvonne had the condo to herself after the wedding. We insisted on a roommate, none of those girls worked out well and Yvonne was happy when at last she got the place to herself.

We had lived in D.C. for two years before the World Bank sent us to the East Africa office in Nairobi, Kenya on a five-year assignment. This assignment meant that for the first time in our lives, we moved away from the children and became empty nesters. Marc married Cherie in 1970 and was living in California. Marian had also moved to California for work. Joan and Yvonne could have come with us but they were both studying at the university.

The 1974 Peugeot – Note the Diplomatic License Plate.

Nairobi, Kenya

Kenya in those years was a wonderful place to live. The World Bank office was rather small and we got to know most of the people well. We became friends, and with some, we are still friends, especially with Laura and John Cleave. Laura, at the time, was not yet married to John. She is quite a character, born in Italy from an Italian father and a Greek mother. She had been married to an American. She carried a United Nations passport, a Greek passport, an Italian Passport and an American Passport! John is an Englishman.

When we arrived in Nairobi, we stayed at first in a hotel. Next door to our suite, there was another newly arrived family, the DuPonts, from the Seychelles. She was American. We got to know them pretty well; the girls were young, four and six years old.

One Sunday afternoon they went on a safari with his parents who were visiting. There was a terrible accident. The car ended up under a truck. All three people in the front seat were decapitated, the father, son and daughter. Driving the roads in Kenya could be disastrous.

We had several adventures with our car, a 1974 Peugeot. The car was only a few weeks old when we went on a Sunday picnic in the Ngong Mountains close to Nairobi. In fact, our cook, Kabuki's family lived there. We met the Nyssen's, Wil, my cousin, Leen and their three children.

*Carla in the Peugeot. It is interesting to note
that the license plate number is etched
onto all the car windows to discourage theft.*

We noticed a dark cloud and decided to pack up and drive home. As we drove home, the rain came down in torrents; the road flooded and we could not get through. We got out of the car, and with the help of the local people, including Yvonne and Joan who were part of a human chain, and we got to dry ground. The men tried to somehow get the cars through the fast raging water. I was scared to death. Paul drove the car. The water came over the hood of the car. Somehow, again with a lot of help, the cars were pushed through.

Carla and Paul in Kenya 1975.

Yvonne remembers her Dad went back about a mile and gunned the car up to about 100 miles per hour and tried to get up enough speed to race through the water. She was part of the human chain that pushed the car as it stalled half way in the river that was coursing over the road. After that, the Peugeot was never the same. The top speed was 25 miles per hour. The mechanics did work on it and it eventually went faster.

Several times we had a flat tire while we visited a game park. It was dangerous to get out of the car while in the park. There was no choice though. I remember one time we had the flat tire on the side of the road very close to a mama lion with her cubs, very relaxed laying there looking at us. We both got out of the car; we left the engine running, so that our human smell was not too obvious. Paul started to change the tire. In the meantime, several cars stopped, both in front of us and behind us. They stayed there until the tire was changed. We thought this was kind and a bit unusual because no one came out of his or her car to help. Not until we had drove off did we see that on the other side of the road, the papa lion was watching us. We changed a tire in between a lion family! Life in Kenya could be exciting.

As a young child, my mother took us very often to Artis, the Amsterdam zoo. I loved it. After Kenya, I cannot stand zoos. I always think about the "poor, cooped up animals!"

In Kenya at that time, the country had its first president by the name of Kenyatta, a charitable leader. Kenya became independent in 1963. People loved him; however, the population was much more tribal than nationally inclined. The tribes were foremost in importance. A Kikuyu would take care of any other Kikuyu. The Kikuyu were the fighters, the landowners and the farmers. The Luo, a more studious people, were the teachers, professors, etc. We were told it was better to have servants from different tribes. If

143

something went wrong or was stolen they would not protect each other.

Carla and Paul in Greece.

Kenya is the place where my life changed. No more children at home. We left them, instead of them leaving us.

We arrived in Kenya late April 1974. Enroute, we spent some vacation days in Athens and on Cypress. A month or so after our visit, Cypress was bombed and the hotel we stayed in was destroyed. Cypress was divided and two governments ruled: the Greeks and the Turks.

Soon after we arrived in Kenya, it was Mother's day. Paul had gone on a "mission," no kids were home and I did not know anybody well enough to spend the day with. I felt very lonely and sorry for myself. I went out and bought myself a silver elephant bracelet. I still have it and when I wear it, it reminds me of that difficult day.

The back yard and house in Nairobi.

Being empty nesters is definitely different, especially for the stay-at-home mother. One has to find something special to do to keep occupied. We moved into a rental house, which was recently built on a street with all new houses. The house had three bedrooms. There were a lot of burglaries all over town. To secure the house we had two watchmen, *askaris* in Swahili, in front and in the back of the house. Also, there was an iron gate that closed off the bedroom section from the rest of the house. When we went to bed we locked it. Even the servants did not have a key. A wonderful British colonial custom is to drink tea first thing in the morning. Kabuki, our steward and cook, would put a tea tray in front of the gate and when we woke up we took it to the bedroom. We continued this custom today and I still have a cup of tea and a biscuit or *ontbijtkoek* the first thing each morning.

The house had servant quarters so we had Kabuki and Charles, a *Kikuju* member of our staff, living with us. However, at night we also had the two *askari*. The best protection was a dog. We had a large garden and again grew our own bananas, papayas, pineapples, avocados, limes, etc. We also had a vegetable garden and we grew our own herbs. The climate in Nairobi is excellent. Even a dead stick in the ground would grow leaves. The gardener refused to weed the garden because that was "women's work" so we had a gal doing the weeding. She was pregnant and delivered her baby right in the garden of another family!

The area used to be an old coffee plantation. On the other side of the street there were still coffee bushes with local cattle freely roaming through it. Our garden at first was not fenced in and our small dog, Sheba, a hunt terrier we acquired from a fellow British World Banker, often ran through those bushes. The result was that the dog had many ticks, which we removed daily, but she often had tick fever, which required treatment by a vet. After the property was fenced, she could not get out and this fixed the problem.

There were also monkeys living around us in the trees and in the bushes. Some local people were bitten by the monkeys and got quite ill. What we called the "monkey disease" turned out to be AIDS. This was our first knowledge and acquaintance with this disease.

On a happier note, we had wonderful neighbors. We used each other's staff when needed for parties. Kitty-corner from us was a large house rented by the U.S. Embassy, and occupied by the Chief Administrative Officer, Charles Brown and his wife, Gigi. They became our lifelong friends. They both passed away in Santa Barbara, California years later.

Sheba (the dog), Paul, Carla and Mama (Jo Olman) relaxing in the back yard in Nairobi.

It was almost impossible to get a telephone installed in Nairobi. Charles, being with the embassy had one. We asked the Browns if they would take messages for us in case of an emergency. On Paul's birthday, Marc called. It was 5 a.m. and Charles, in his pajamas came over and tried to wake us up. He finally did succeed.

Gigi Brown introduced me to the American Women's Club. My job was to visit the sick American tourists in the hospital. There were some real sob stories. Several times I had to ask help from the embassy to get sick people an extended visa or financial help with airline tickets, which had expired, or money to buy food. Once we ourselves bought a return ticket for someone. Fortunately, we were paid back.

I also worked with the Kenyan Red Cross. I had to teach basic hygiene to local women. It was better to use newspaper in the baby's basket than nothing. I also taught the importance of what to feed the children once they stopped nursing. As in Liberia, many children under the age of three died from the wrong diet and malnutrition, not hunger.

I had two surgeries while in Nairobi in the Kenyatta hospital. The surgeon was from South Africa and very well trained indeed. Before Idi Amin took over in Uganda, one of the best medical schools in Africa was in Uganda. When I had a hysterectomy, I was in the President's room, which was unbelievably large, clean and well-serviced with private nursing care. I was lucky that they had two such rooms in that special wing of the hospital. I would have been kicked out if one of Kenyatta's family members had needed it. Actually, I was also in that room for my knee surgery.

Gigi and I would get together for cooking lessons. My expertise was in Indonesian food. We would be in my kitchen or hers with eight or so other women. Afterwards we would eat whatever we had prepared.

Carla and her mother, Jo Olman at the Equator.

As I wrote above, we had a good size garden and were mostly self sufficient with fruit and vegetables. In the afternoon before dinner I would go with Kabuki into the garden and decide what vegetable to eat. It was fun cooking over there. I needed only to cook. Kabuki did the cutting, cleaning, etc. and cleaned up all the pots and pans I used. The only problem was to adjust the recipes to 5,280 feet above sea level (the altitude of Nairobi is the same as Denver, Colorado).

My mother visited us there several times. She loved it. The servants, like all Kenyans, have a great respect for old age. They catered to her every wish and she had no trouble talking with them in pigeon English. She was very shy with the English language and our friends.

Joan, Marian, Carla and Yvonne in Nairobi.

We had some good Dutch friends, the Niemantsverdriets. Rosemarie Niemantsverdriet died a few years ago, but I am still in contact with Paul, her husband and Sandra, her daughter who lives in Florida. Paul Niemantsverdriet visits his daughter in Florida every year at Christmastime. We were also friends with Paul and Helen Borchert from the Nairobi Hilton where Paul Borchert was the general manager. Fifteen years later, Paul Borchert arranged the reception for our 45th Wedding Anniversary in Amsterdam. It was a *rijsttafel* at the Schiphol Hilton, where he worked in Amsterdam.

Appie Mof and Miep (Carla's sister)
also came to visit in Kenya.

Onetime all three girls came to visit. That was wonderful. We went to Mombasa and also went on different safaris. Yvonne and Joan came twice a year as long as they were students at Georgetown and the World Bank paid for a yearly trip. I did consulting (for no pay) for K.L.M. airlines and I only needed to pay 50% of the price of each ticket. So we made one ticket into two! It worked like a charm; all of this was First Class travel.

While we lived in Kenya, Paul and I lost three parents. Paul's mother died May 1, 1975. Paul had gone to see her a few months before. I still regret he was not there when she passed away. Paul's father died March 1, 1977. Paul was in Rwanda when I received a letter from Hannie, his sister. In this letter she wrote that medically speaking they could not understand why he was still alive. All of a sudden it hit me, "He was waiting for Paul." Paul was his favorite son. I sent a telex to Paul who received it only when he boarded the plane in Kigali. This was on a Friday afternoon. I had made reservations for him for the Friday midnight flight on K.L.M. to Holland. He came home at 7 p.m. changed to warm clothes, repacked his suitcase and flew to Holland. He saw his father at 8 a.m. on Saturday morning and his father died peacefully at noon that day.

My mother passed away on June 23, 1977, the same year that Paul's father died. My mother had visited us the year before in the States to attend both Marian and Joan's weddings. She had had a wonderful time. She flew First Class and was treated royally wherever she went. She told me that this was the first time in the twelve years after my father's death that she really and truly enjoyed herself.

After the weddings we went to Holland in August to celebrate her 80th birthday. This time she let everyone know that she was one year younger than my father. She was always very vague about her age. For years she always said she was three years younger than Papa. In 1946 on her birthday she was staying in a hotel in Den Haag and she asked me to pick up her passport and bring it to her. Of course, I looked in the passport and realized she was 50 years old that day. I bought 50 roses and went over there and said, "This is a special birthday" in front of her friends. She could have murdered me!

*Carla, Mama (Jo Olman) and Yvonne on Safari
in Kenya in 1977.*

In February and March of 1977, she again came to Kenya to visit us. I saw her in Holland in the beginning of June. She seemed to be fine, though apparently she felt nervous and depressed. The doctor had over-prescribed Valium for her. She became very confused; she did not know morning from evening. My niece Ellen decided she had to be hospitalized. Miep was on vacation with Appie in Portugal. They flew home and I came from Nairobi. I visited her for a few days. We were told by the nurse she was dying. Her doctor of many years was on vacation. I was also told that she would get a shot to relax her. That evening she passed away. I do not know if my mother asked for that medicine or that she was aware of it. I know she was ready to go. Those things can happen in Holland.

During our time while we lived in Kenya two of our daughters married. Marian married Bob Cummings on June 5, 1976 in California and Joan married Pat Conner at the National Audubon Society in Chevy Chase, Maryland on July 4, 1976. They thought it was a terrific day to get married but it was difficult because everything was closed for the Bicentennial. It was hard to get a caterer and we ended up with the caterer from the White House.

When Marian and Bob decided to marry, Bob wrote a letter to Paul to ask for Marian's hand in marriage. Paul wrote back and asked how many cows would Bob offer for Marian, as was the Kenyan custom. Bob replied he had no cattle but would let Paul borrow his golf clubs.

Joan graduated from Georgetown University in Business Administration in May 1976. She originally wanted to study Medicine. Joan loves to help other people. On our way back to Nairobi following the two weddings and graduation, we stopped in Holland and helped Mama celebrate her 80th birthday as mentioned earlier. In four months time, we had four major events that summer of 1976.

We had rented a house in Bethesda because our own house was rented out. I was rather exhausted and within a few weeks upon our return to Nairobi, I lost my memory. The episode lasted about seven hours. Paul was very concerned and I was sent to London for a brain scan and other tests. Nothing was found and the doctors decided I must have had a broken blood vessel in the brain. Fortunately, it was a one-time occasion.

I went on quite a few trips with Paul. One of the reasons was that the World Bank had a point system. When the World Bank officer was on a business trip outside the U.S., the spouse earned one point for every night that officer was away from home. When 200 points were earned, the spouse could go along and the airfare was paid for. After 300 points everything was paid for; airfare, hotel and food.

Paul traveled so often that I had quite a few trips with him! The one I remember best was to the Comoros, Madagascar and the Seychelles. The Comoro Islands were independent after a long period of French colonization. In my experience, it was the poorest place we ever visited. Paul went there because of an infestation of rats. They were completely taking over all agricultural crops, mainly the coconuts. The coconuts were important because they were one of the few things they had going for them. The French had completely supported the islands. After the French left there was no income, no crops, and no industry. The only thing in abundance was lobster. So people ate lobster for breakfast, lunch and dinner. There was no wheat, very little sugar, and they were very short on drinking water and power, etc. The government had recently been taken over by some very young soldiers who had no inkling how to run a country. They came to power through a coup d'état.

The story was so similar to a novel, which was published around that time, _The Dogs of War_ by Frederick Forsyth. Everyone was wondering if they had initiated the story out of that book. From the Comoros, we went to Madagascar, another rather underdeveloped nation, though fortunately they have improved their country a great deal. One of the things the World Bank was interested in was the Ylang-Ylang trees. The flowers of the tree are processed by distillation then the essential oil is extracted and used as a base for expensive perfumes and more recently medications. A small bottle costs hundreds of dollars. The plants grow along the Cananga tree trunks in a dense wooded area. The system of extracting the liquid was very primitive. I believe the World Bank financed the modernization process.

We flew from Madagascar to the Seychelles for rest and relaxation for five days or so. When we had unpacked, we were told to immediately return to Nairobi. We were not sure why. There was not a taxi to be found. One car was leaving the resort, they took us halfway to the airport, dumped us and the luggage on the side of the road and that was it. Fortunately, after an hour or so someone else came by and took us to the airport. There were only two flights a week to Kenya and the hour of departure had long since passed. However, the plane had not left because it had not yet arrived. After several hours of waiting; it arrived and we could board. The plane had very narrow canvas seats, no air pressurization and no toilet. We could only fly at 8,000 feet. It was scary but a wonderful way to see the coastline of Tanzania and Kenya. We landed in Nairobi (which is over 5000 feet), worn out but in one piece. I do not remember if I was airsick. I am sure of it though.

We lived almost five years in Nairobi and they were good years. Unfortunately, Paul's asthma returned, he apparently was allergic to dust, cockroaches and pyrethrum, a plant, which grows in large fields around Nairobi.

We could have extended our stay but with Paul's health we did not. Another interesting experience we had over there was with the IRS. Someone in the Pretoria office of the U.S. government decided to audit us over three years. Of course, we did not bring with us any of the supporting tax papers. Somehow the man came every three months or so with the necessary correspondence in between to ask us for other details. It became a terrible nuisance. The bickering was over $64.00. Imagine what it cost to fly from Pretoria to Nairobi, stay at hotels and eat, all over a disputed $64.00! We finally complained to the Embassy in Nairobi. We never saw the man again and we got $32.00 back!

While in Nairobi, I continued to work as an outside consultant for the real estate company where I had worked previously in the D.C. area. I provided referrals to the company. I really enjoyed selling real estate at that time. Before we left for Nairobi, I was rather successful at selling. After our five year assignment and our return to the World Bank Headquarters in D.C., I was offered a real estate management-training course, but somehow, my interest was not there anymore and I declined.

Carla and Paul at Wolftrap Farm in Virginia.

Back in D.C.

We returned to Washington, D.C. in 1979. I became active with the World Bank International Volunteer Services (WIVES). In 1983, I became the President. We changed the name to World Bank Volunteer Services (WBVS). Two years ago, the name was changed again to World Bank Family Network (WBFN). The organization has grown a lot and has the full support of the World Bank.

In my time, we had to fight for privileges for the spouses'. A spouse could not get a World Bank I.D. unless the husband approved. No medical treatment could be paid for unless the husband signed the insurance form. Spouses in a divorce settlement could not use most bank privileges.

The bank would only talk to the employee; this was also the same for pension plans. Fortunately, slowly but surely, all this has changed for the better.

Carla is third from the right at a meeting of The World Bank Volunteer Services' past presidents reunion. Washington, D.C.

The Volunteer Services had an office with an administrator and secretary, all paid for by the bank. The administrator in my time was Natalie W., hired by the personnel department. At first things went well, but she became more and more a bank person and less and less interested in the volunteers even though they worked hard and did a lot of things. She had no respect for them. It all came to a head and she and the secretary resigned. After lots of discussion we were allowed to interview applicants for the job and we could decide whom we wanted. It all ended up very positive and the organization has thrived.

After my term was over, I needed to do something, which held my interest.

So I decided to become a paralegal. I had realized my interest in the law while I was in the real estate business. I enrolled in a course given at George Washington University. I only followed a few classes at the time because I had also joined the law firm of Lee Holdman. Years before I had sold him a house and we had kept in contact. I only worked part time. The firm mainly specialized in estate and tax planning. I enjoyed this very much. Paul was traveling a lot and it kept me busy.

Upon our return from Kenya, Paul had joined the IFC (International Finance Company) the private lending arm of the World Bank.

The Raleigh bike still rolling
in 2015 – 35 years later!

160

Paul traveled a great deal, though officially an employee was not supposed to travel more than 120 days in a calendar year. There were several times that Paul had to travel to Europe twice a week. He was allowed to fly on the Concord because it was less tiring. The Concord made the trip from Paris to Washington, D.C. in two and a half hours!

On one of those Concord flights he brought home a Raleigh bicycle for me. He had bought the bike at Harrods's in London, put it in a cab, drove to the airport and put it on the flight. I had this bike a long time. A very special one!

In 1981, Paul had back surgery. A growth was pressing on his spine. Just before he was hospitalized, President Ronald Reagan was shot along with James Brady, his White House Press secretary. Brady was confined in the room next to Paul at George Washington hospital. We became friendly with the Secret Service agents on duty. We also met Brady's wife. We exchanged cookies though we never saw Brady himself. A few years later, Paul had prostate cancer. This time the surgery was performed at Georgetown University Hospital. It was 1987. The surgery was successful except that it lasted a very long time and I was a nervous wreck. He needed many pints of blood. His recuperation was hampered by high fevers in and out of the hospital. He had the surgery in October. November, a month later, on our 40th wedding anniversary he was in the hospital again. It took months of recuperation time. He decided during that time to stop working and retire. He went on an extended leave of absence with full pay and his official retirement was on his 65th birthday. He did consulting for the World

Bank for several years afterwards. We decided to leave Washington D.C. after that.

This was a very difficult decision for me because I really liked living in D.C. Paul hated the climate. Just before he stopped his official work we went on a round the world trip for the World Bank. We traveled to Indonesia, Thailand, Denmark, Italy, Switzerland and Holland.

Carla and Paul in 1993
after travelling the world.

Around the World

Because of Paul's extensive travel, being away from home and accumulation of travel points, I was invited to join Paul on his extended around the world trip in 1986.

In Denmark, we visited several plants which manufactured power producing windmills. Paul was anxious for the World Bank to get involved in producing cheap electricity for developing countries and now they do.

In Italy, we were in Turin visiting FIAT tractor plants. He had to go to Geneva and we were given a Fiat car with a chauffeur, this car was fully lined with ultra suede. Amazing!

The trip to the Fiat factory was at the time that Italy was a finalist in the World Cup Soccer Tournament. The game was played in Mexico. Everyone wanted to watch the game. The Fiat people who were assigned to entertain us for dinner were told that they had not been given a choice. I remember that dinner very well. A fancy restaurant and we were the only table occupied! The waiter came to tell us every five minutes the progress of the game. Our meal consisted of 12 different courses, all with various varieties of mushrooms. Italy lost. The restaurant filled up and our hosts relaxed!

After the business in Italy was finished, we spent a few days in a hotel in Largo Maggiore in Northern Italy's Po Valley. We had been there years before in a small hotel "Lido La Perla Nero." It was still there. We also were there one time with Miep and Appie. It is a lovely lake and a wonderful, relaxing vacation spot, except this time Paul was called to Milan for some business. I stayed by myself, which was not the idea.

While we were in Turin, Italy our suitcases were packed in the car, which was parked in the sun all day. When I opened the suitcases the clothes came out wrinkled as if the wrinkles had been ironed in by the heat!

On one of the other trips I made with Paul, I believe it was to Thailand and Indonesia; we first stopped in Albuquerque to visit Yvonne in Gallup and to meet Michael. Yvonne had a small car; our luggage did not fit in it. Paul left his suitcases in storage (or so we thought) at the Albuquerque Airport. Two days later upon our return, the suitcases were gone, stolen obviously. After Albuquerque, we went to Twin Falls where we bought suitcases, underwear, socks, and pajamas. Suits and radio, etc. were purchased in Hong Kong. In those years in Hong Kong they could sew suits and safari outfits in 24 hours or less!! The real problem was all his World Bank working papers. His secretary teletyped most of the necessary papers to us. It was quite an experience.

Life was exciting while we travelled but I was always happy to get home again. Of all the places I lived and visited, I enjoyed life in D.C. the most.

House in Potomac, Maryland.

The Potomac House

I already mentioned that I liked living in the D.C. area. I found it a stimulating place. So much was happening. There were so many opportunities to see things and to take part in events. I visited the White House several times and once had lunch with then First Lady, Barbara Bush. We attended Senate hearings, museum openings and Washington National Symphony concerts both in the Kennedy Center and in the park on the 4th of July. I entertained a lot of foreign guests for the World Bank-IMF, especially during the G-7 Summit. At yearly meetings of the Group of Seven, I met dignitaries and the wives of presidents.

My friends were from many different nationalities. We had an African book club and I enjoyed reading and discussing books by African authors. I no longer have the book list, but suffice it to say, I felt very much part of the International Washington scene.

Later on I did miss this in Colorado Springs, however, after awhile we met nice people who became close friends there. Yvonne had warned me once that so many of my Washington friends were not American and eventually they would leave to retire to their home countries or that I would lose them, and that it was better to have American friends.

The townhouse in Potomac was a three-story townhouse, a good size home with a double car garage which separated one house from the next house. The houses were around a courtyard. Our court was only two-sided. The common area was grass, plants and trees, and was taken care of by the homeowners association.

For a number of years, Paul was in charge of the architectural committee. What a headache that was! People were unhappy if they were told "No, you cannot have a red front door and you need to ask permission to change the paint color." It was a rather unique set up and quite a few people were interested in living there. Over the years we received many notes in our mailbox with the request to contact the person if and when we decided to sell the house.

I saved one of the last notes, and after Paul's illness, followed by our decision to move away from the Washington, D.C. area, I sent a note to that person. This

167

was in the beginning of January 1988. She immediately contacted us and three weeks later we had a contract. She wanted to move into the house in July and we had no idea where we were going to move to.

On one of our many long airplane trips, Paul had figured out that the geographical center of the places where our children lived was Denver. This was before Marc moved to Colorado and was still living in Idaho. The distance calculation was not really correct because Marian and Bob were in Spokane in Washington State.

We considered Santa Fe because of the cultural scene. We made a trip to Santa Fe. We looked at Santa Fe and drove from there to Colorado, which was so much lovelier; green and lush. We were also concerned about the 7,000-foot altitude of Santa Fe. Also, in Denver there was the National Jewish Medical Center, the foremost lung and allergy research center in the U.S. Our doctor, Dr. Fidler, in Washington, D.C. had urged Paul to become a patient there. Marc and Cherie lived in Boulder, we would have liked to go there, however, we knew that they were unhappy together and we did not want to be in the middle of it. They divorced. Marc and his second wife, Karen married in September 1992 in Denver. In those years Denver often had a big brown cloud hanging over it during much of the winter. We were concerned about the air quality in Denver, so we chose Colorado Springs.

Quite a few years before, when we picked up a Mercedes in Twin Falls to drive it to Potomac, we drove south since the weather was bad. We went south of Denver to go east on Highway 50. We stopped in Colorado Springs and had lunch at the Broadmoor Hotel. We walked around a bit and I fell in love with the neighborhood. I remember thinking that it would be nice to live there.

That same trip took us through Kansas, Garden City, Dodge City and Kingman. We had no idea that Joan and Pat would live in Kingman, Kansas. A few years later we decided Colorado Springs was a pretty good place to live.

Colorado Spring, Colorado.

Home in Colorado Springs

In the end we decided, as I said previously, on Colorado Springs. We looked again and could not find a house which suited us. So we bought a lot in the Broadmoor neighborhood. We designed the outline of the house on a napkin. The house plans were drawn up and we selected a builder, Larry Nichols.

When we purchased the lot, the seller of the lot had a house for sale next door. We rented that house during the building of our new home. It was an old steel frame house purchased from the 1933 Chicago World Fair. It was cold, poorly designed and hardly insulated. We moved in August 1988. The builder started with our house in

September of that year. It was finished in May 1989. We moved in just before Mother's Day.

While the house was being built, Paul really enjoyed living next door, because every morning when we woke up he could see if the workmen were there. He watched every detail of the house being built. He spent a lot of time over at the worksite and he loved it.

The house was our dream house because we designed it with having in mind how our furniture, carpets and books would fit in, how we liked to entertain, how we needed enough space for children and grandchildren's visits and Paul's love for gardening. After so many moves and living in so many different countries on four different continents. It was perfect.

We lived in it together until December 22, 2001 when Paul had a pontine stroke six hours after he came home from the hospital after quadruple bypass heart surgery on December 18th. I lived in it for another two and a half years.

When we moved to Colorado Springs in 1988, we did not know anybody there and since we had no more children at home and Paul was retired it was more difficult to get to know people.

One of the first things we did was to visit the Symphony House, the office of the Colorado Springs Symphony Association. We learned about the guild, the programs they had, etc. In September, I attended a guild meeting. I heard at that meeting that there was also an evening support group called "Encore." We went that same evening to that meeting and that was the beginning of a close relationship with the Symphony. Paul became a board member. He ended up serving nine years on the board. Towards the end, he became disenchanted with them, mainly because of poor financial management. He felt the Israeli conductor, Yakie Bergman, was treated very badly. Yakie and Paul became very good friends. Several years after Paul resigned from the board; the Symphony had to file for bankruptcy and ceased to exist. Paul was right to be concerned.

My involvement was mainly with the Colorado Springs Opera Festival. The house we rented while building our home and the lot we bought belonged to Jackie Ostheimer, a wealthy woman, who had had at least three husbands. She never lived in Colorado Springs, only vacationed there. She was kind enough to introduce us to Terri and Elizabeth Lilly. Elizabeth was the Administrative Director for the Colorado Springs Opera Festival. They invited us first to lunch and later to a cocktail party at their house where we met Don Jenkins and his wife. Don was the general and artistic director of Colorado Springs Opera Festival. He also was a professor at Colorado College and he was the founder of the opera company. I became involved first with the guild and later as President of the guild with the company itself. As President of the guild I was on the Opera Festival company board. I became Vice President of that board and later the President. I attended an annual meeting of Opera America in Seattle.

After that meeting, Opera America invited me to become a member of a committee. It was a newly formed committee whose task was to study the role of Opera America and what role it could and should play for trustees and volunteers in the opera world. Opera America for years had been the National Organization to assist professional opera people. We met four times a year for two years. It was fun and productive. Opera America now has a whole division for trustees and volunteers and works closely with Opera Volunteers International, formerly known as Opera Guilds International. I met many people from all over the country, who were active in the opera world.

*Paul and Carla at one of their
many opera guild galas.*

Between the symphony and the opera, Paul and I did get well acquainted with people in Colorado Springs who had the same interests. We had many meetings at our house. With some planning, we could fit 50 people in the house. Thirty people were easier to accommodate. For several years we offered and cooked an Indonesian *Rijsttafel* as a fundraiser. People paid $50.00 to attend. All of this money went to the opera. On the average we would serve 12 people, though one time we had 18 for a sit down dinner.

The first time we did this, we were able to entertain the guests with a real Indonesian Gamelan orchestra. An Indonesian professor with Colorado College music students performed on the gamelan instruments the college owned. It was great, though they were disappointed that we did not offer them all the *Rijsttafel* food. I had told them that I would only make them *Nasi Goreng*, the fried rice, but the professor did not like that. He made so much trouble afterwards that I had to call the head of the department.

For many years the Opera Guild held an antique show at the Broadmoor hotel. It involved professional dealers, old beautiful antiques, jewelry, furniture, etc. Paul became in charge. It was a big job. It took months to get the dealers, write contracts, arrange with the hotel, the security people, line up the volunteers, etc. He did a terrific job. On the average, we made between $15,000 and $25,000. It was a good fundraiser. In 1999 during the Opera Guild's International yearly convention, which took place that year in Denver, we both received the Opera Volunteer of the Year Award. This was quite an honor!

Life was busy, but enjoyable. The first three years after we moved to Colorado Springs, Paul still traveled a great deal because he did consulting work for the World Bank. After awhile he realized how tiring the work and the travel was, and fortunately, he did not continue doing this work.

In Washington, D.C., I had received my paralegal degree through the courses I took at George Washington University Law School. I loved it and graduated cum laude.

After arriving in Colorado Springs, I got a job as a volunteer paralegal with Pikes Peak Legal Services, a federally supported Colorado State legal aid program for those people who could not afford an attorney. I did Public Benefit cases. I worked mainly with people who were denied Medicaid and/or disability coverage because of a mental or physical disability. It was interesting, some people really needed it, and others tried to take advantage of the system. I was also involved with landlord and tenant cases, living wills, etc. My two days a week often became three or four days a week. I did not mind.

The preparation to advocate in front of an administrative law judge took many hours. I did this for nine years, and then I got burned out. I was losing patience with the clients whose cases were not always legitimate, who tried to take advantage of the system and who tried to get benefits they should not get. I decided to quit. I also did not care for the new director. Working at Legal Services gave me another perspective on life. It made me realize how privileged our lives are. It was good to be able to help others.

I lived for 16 years in Colorado Springs from August 1988 to August 2004. We lived in the house at 52 Broadmoor Avenue starting in May 1989. Paul, sadly enough, was there for only 13 years. During our married life, it was the longest time we lived in one house. We were also the happiest there. There was pressure from some of the volunteer work we did, but no more work pressure, not any more of those long tiring trips.

*Carla's Surprise 70th Birthday Party at Marc and Karen's home
in Cherry Creek, Colorado.*

Carla, Paul and Miep in Fort Myers Beach, Florida.

We led a busy social life and we enjoyed it. For a number of years, we spent several winter months in Fort Myers Beach, Florida, where we purchased a share in Marc's apartment.

While living in Colorado Springs, Paul, indeed, became a patient at National Jewish Medical Center in Denver. His asthma came under control, though he developed some other lung problems. We made many visits to Denver. I also became a patient at National Jewish Medical Center because of a consistent cough. I was diagnosed with chronic bronchitis, Chronic Obstructive Pulmonary Disease (COPD). National Jewish was started in the late 1890s. At first, patients, mainly children, were treated free of charge. However, in later years this became impossible. Patients were charged.

National Jewish does a lot of research and they have to do major fundraising. We got involved and we gave several cocktail parties at the house to introduce National Jewish to our friends and acquaintances. I was asked to become a National Trustee. Later after I moved to Spokane, I hosted one event, a luncheon, since I am still a Trustee of National Jewish.

Paul and I became very much part of Colorado Spring's society. Our friends were mainly among people who also enjoyed the symphony and the opera. We also were part of an investment club. Many clubs were started during the mid 1990s.

The last of many Father's Day Family Reunions in Boulder, Colorado in 2001.

We first started one with about 18 women, called the M&M's (Money & Mrs. – or make out of it what you want). As usual, only a few persons were very active in it. However, we all learned a lot about the stock market and the companies we invested in. We did not make much money, but the social and learning aspect worked well. We existed for three years and then our treasurer, Ursula Bird, moved to Arizona and there was no one to take over from her so we dissolved.

However, some of us decided to form another investment club together with spouses. The name became M&M2. Paul was the treasurer and I was the presiding partner. I found it interesting to observe the difference in the approach of the buying and selling of stocks. Men are

179

much more risk takers than women. Most of the time I disagreed to sell, I found it too early; after one studies a company and one invests in it, there are good reasons to hold on to it and give it a chance. The ups and downs of the market are always there!

Marian, Yvonne, Paul and Joan in Colorado Springs.

Colorado Springs was a good choice for us. We were always happy when the kids came to visit. Joan and Pat and their five offspring would come. They often drove through the night. The kids would sleep and the traffic was light. The result was that they arrived at 3 a.m. or so. And after they arrived we would talk. So those nights none of us slept much. Kingman was 420 miles away. Yvonne and Michael were about 520 miles away. Marc lived a 100 miles away and Marian and Bob 1200 miles away. They had to fly in.

We traveled to the children and they in turn came to see us. It was great and it was exactly what we had hoped would happen.

The house was not only perfect for company, but also for house guests. The two bedrooms and two sitting rooms downstairs could sleep seven or eight people. We had it built with that in mind, that the children and grandchildren could visit and stay and have their own space to spread out.

Paul loved the garden. When we built the house, we had extensive landscaping done. However, over the years, he did lots of improvements. The first fall we planted 600 tulip bulbs, mainly in front and on the side of the house. We learned very fast that this was a mistake. The deer loved them. As soon as the tulips started blooming they were eaten! From then on Paul planted the tulips in the fenced back garden. He spent many, many hours in the garden with the help of Janek, a young man from Poland. They planted many roses, Paul's favorite plant. He did it in memory of his mother who was also very fond of roses.

My most favorite holiday is Thanksgiving Day. We both very much liked to have the children with us and to have a long leisurely meal with lots of talk. The last one with Paul we actually had the Sunday before Thanksgiving, because Karen and Marc were going to Florida to celebrate the day with Karen's parents in Fort Myers Beach. It was a month before Paul's stroke and death. Yvonne and family and our oldest granddaughter Johanna was also with us.

The following year, Thanksgiving 2002, I wanted everyone to be there. Not all of them could make it. Marc,

Karen, Joan and Pat with some of their offspring were there.

I moved to Spokane to be close to Marian and Bob in August 2004. The Colorado Springs' house was sold in October of that year. We had many happy times in that house. We had made many, many good friends. The house had large rooms; it was well built and very comfortable. In the beginning I thought it was too big for us, but I got used to it very quickly.

Carla on her 80ᵀᴴ Birthday.

Spokane, Washington

Moving to Spokane started a new chapter in my life. There were several reasons for this move. I was all by myself in a large house surrounded by a good-sized garden. I could handle the house, I could not take care of the garden and it was difficult to give it the tender loving care Paul had given it.

I also got quite ill with the Chronic Bronchitis I have and there was a heart problem in 2003. A stent was put into one of my arteries. After Paul died, Marian came to Colorado Springs at least nine times in eighteen months to help me.

It was the children's decision that I should move. The most logical place was Spokane. For me it was difficult to agree with their suggestion. Leaving Colorado Springs, good friends, the house, everything I knew so well and also I realized that it would be less frequent that I would see Marc and Karen, Joan and Pat, Yvonne and Michael and all their families. It is much harder and further to travel to Spokane when compared to Colorado Springs. I am sad it turned out this way but having Marian and Bob close by makes up for this. They are wonderful for me. The irony of my move is also that my granddaughters, Jo and Lacey and their families moved to Denver after I moved away. Yvonne and Michael are also now living close to Denver.

Carla's house on Blue Fern Lane at Rockwood South Retirement Center in Spokane, Washington.

One nice way to visit with family has been that for the last decade I have spent several weeks during the winter in the south, most often in Florida on Fisher Island where Marc and Karen have their beautiful apartment.

It took about a year to adjust to life in Spokane. The house, which was built to my specification, was about a third of the size of the Colorado Springs house. It was very well appointed. I had close neighbors who have become good friends. The Rockwood Retirement Community is a good and caring place to live. One can be very busy with the programs they offer including bridge clubs, book clubs and exercise programs. The security is good.

Spokane is a lovely city. There is a good symphony and was a not so good opera. The opera asked me to be on their board, but I resigned within the year. The people were hard to have a rapport with. All they wanted was money.

Recently plans for a new opera company have started up. I wish them well and hope it will be great.

After I arrived in Spokane, I immediately joined the Spokane Chapter of Hadassah. I transferred my membership from the Colorado Springs Chapter. It enabled me to meet many wonderful women right away.

Less than a year later I was asked to join the board and not long after that I was voted in as President of the Chapter. This kept me quite busy as President for three years and I am still very supportive of Hadassah. As President, I also attended meetings of the Pacific Northwest chapter in Seattle. I also took part in the annual meetings in different cities.

I really enjoyed getting to know so many different women and hearing all about their endeavors for Hadassah.

Spokane Hadassah board 2007: Lynn Soss, Carolyn Ellis, Lucy
Gipstein, Carla Peperzak, Lois Rubens, Sue Glass,
Miriam Abramowitz, and Julie Morris.

I also became a board member of the Reform
congregation "Beth Haverim." At the time there were two
small Reform congregations in Spokane. I was on the board
when we voted to combine the two congregations. The
name was changed to Congregation EmanuEl. I am still a
member. I also am a member of Temple Beth Shalom, the
conservative congregation. I was on the Spokane Jewish
Family Services board, too.

While I was living in Spokane, in November 2006,
Appie, my sister's husband, had a stroke. He lived several
weeks and then he died. My sister, Miep passed away in
April 2014.

*Miep, Carla and Jopie Markus-Cats "The Three Sisters" just
before Miep passed away in April, 2014.*

I met and became friends with Eva Lassman. Eva was a
Holocaust survivor from the camps. She had been telling
her story for many years in schools around the area. She
was a good educator. However she had to stop giving
lectures because of ill health.

She continued to be a member of the Yom Hashoah
committee, where I had become a member as well.

I was asked to talk about my experiences. We did
several presentations together until she was not able to do
this any longer.

I sort of took her place, though my story is very different
when compared to her story. She was in several death
camps and talked about her experiences there.

The Holocaust Center for Humanity in Seattle asked me to become a member of their Speakers' Bureau.

In 2017, I gave 26 presentations. I am able to do this because my daughter Marian is helping me. She not only drives me, she handles the computers, reminds me if I forget something and altogether she is my right hand.

The first time I was asked to talk about my experiences during the war, was in Colorado by a private school teacher at the Colorado Springs School. The students were rehearsing a play, "The Diary of Anne Frank." The teacher believed the students would have a better understanding of what happened during those years if a person who had lived through that time could talk to them about it and explain what took place during the war.

One of the students in the cast was the daughter of a good friend who knew that I had lived close to the Frank family. I only spoke to the cast and the supporting staff. Over the years, I have talked to other students who were going to perform a play or a musical program on the Holocaust. Afterwards I always get an invitation to attend the performance. Most of the time I decline to attend, because even after so many years, it is still difficult for me to watch it.

The second time I told my story was in Spokane. I was still living in Colorado Springs and planned to visit Marian and her family. My granddaughter Megan asked me to tell my story in her school while I was visiting. I remember how I agonized beforehand on what to say and how to say it.

These days, I do not agonize any more, but I never really look forward to a presentation. However, if the audience is really listening and trying to grasp all the terrible happenings of those years, I feel encouraged even though I never feel satisfied that I have done a good enough job.

It is impossible to put into words and to explain what it really felt like to live during that time. To lose your friends one by one, your close relatives, not to know if they were in hiding, in camps or killed. Towards the end of the war we were really hungry and we were scared all the time.

After every talk, I am exhausted and glad it is over and at the same time grateful that I am able to do this. I feel all of this is worthwhile for two reasons. It is important that I do this, because so many people have never heard about the Holocaust, or they do not believe it happened or that it was as terrible as it was. The second reason for me is that I want to make sure that my relatives and friends and all the other victims are remembered. As long as I am able, I will try to do my part to tell the story.

Before giving a talk I always pray to God to help me convey the importance of remembering. When I talk to schools, I always end with the word respect, because I think if we can learn to respect one another, we can't kill.

All the Peperzak cousins:
Jean Lenglet, Kee Arens, Jenneke Arens, Ad Lenglet (not
pictured), Frans Lenglet, Josien Arens, Marc Peperzak, Pedro
Arens, Paula Arens, Marian Peperzak, Hans Arens, Margriet
Lenglet, Koos Arens, Joan Peperzak, Corien Arens, Yvonne
Peperzak, Maria Arens, Vera Lenglet, Mirjam Lenglet, Vincent
Arens (not pictured), Bas Arens, Liesbeth Arens.

Utrecht, The Netherlands May 2017

My son, Marc and his wife, Karen initiated the idea to have a Peperzak cousins' reunion. He also generously offered to foot the bill. Between them Paul's sisters had 19 children: Corrie had 12 children and Hannie had seven children. Paul and I had four children. All but two of the cousins and their partners attended the event. I was also invited and so were Ad and Angela, Paul's brother and his wife, though we are of the older generation. It turned out to be a fabulously successful event.

Marian kept track of the attendees and Gilbert Horbach, my grandnephew (Miep's grandson), did an amazing job of organizing the hotel and all the events, the boat tour, the bicycle trip, the walking tour and the meals. It was so very special to see everybody and to meet their spouses/partners; 48-hours of getting reacquainted, revisiting old memories and getting updated on everyone's lives, etc.

Gilbert had also organized an Olman family reunion, a much smaller and different afternoon affair. However, for me it was very meaningful, also full of memories, many sad ones and at the same time gratefulness for lives saved and well lived.

It was amazing to meet again after so many years, my two nieces, Mieke and Wilma, who were one and three, when I helped them and their parents (my Aunt Fie and Uncle Lo) to go into hiding. There was no way to have babies and small children in hiding so we had to separate the children from their parents. We placed the children with foster families. The foster families would tell the neighbors that the children were their nieces and nephews and had come to live with them.

Wilma thanked me again for saving her life. The first time I saved her life was when she went into hiding.

I had forgotten the second time. This was after the war when she was living as a daughter with a loving couple. No one knew her real name and the possibility of finding her real parents was nil. She was given a new name in hiding. She was taught to use only the new name, Willie Bakker. She learned her lesson well and forgot her given name. Wilma was moved while in hiding. She was so young that she had no idea who her parents were. Her parents had no idea where she was.

After the liberation her parents asked me to find Wilma, who was about six and a half. I requested the help of a Canadian officer and his jeep. I was asking people within the network if they knew where she was. I knew approximately where she had been in hiding. I went to one home and asked and they would send me to another home where there had been children in hiding. At one point we stopped and a group of children surrounded us.

Imagine driving very slowly through neighborhoods in a Canadian jeep. The children would gather around because they knew they would get candy. Wilma was in a group of children around our jeep and suddenly pointed to me and said, "Carla?"

She was found!

The amazing part of this is that I went with her to her loving foster parents and they allowed me to take her to her parents! She is still in contact with her foster parents, who she calls her uncle and aunt. She nominated them and their names were accepted for the "Righteous Among the Nations," an official title awarded by Yad Vashem on behalf of the State of Israel and the Jewish people to non-Jews who risked their lives to save Jews from extermination by the nazies.

Mieke and Wilma in 1941-1942. Mieke, Carla and Wilma, 76 years later at the Olman Reunion in Utrecht.

Carla's Apartment at Rockwood South.

The Present

I am now 94 years old and live in an apartment. Rockwood South Hill built a beautiful eleven-story apartment building where I moved from my home of twelve years on Blue Fern Lane in the Forest Estates of Rockwood South Hill.

At first, I was hesitant to move. It was a huge undertaking and meant another move and change in my life. However, I am happy I made the decision. I am grateful to be living in a beautiful place.

The staff is very caring and helpful. I made new friends and my social life is great and sometimes overwhelming. I am so busy! Most dinners are eaten in one of the dining rooms downstairs and are fun. We sit around and talk for hours.

I play bridge, attend lectures, swim and attend many of the exercise classes. I am also active in two Jewish Congregations in town, Temple Beth Shalom and Congregation EmanuEl, though not as much as before. Age is catching up! I still drive my Lexus in the neighborhood but only in the daytime and in good weather!

Carla on her 94th Birthday – 2017.

Fortunately, I am still able to give talks in schools and organizations about my experiences during the Holocaust. I could not do this without the assistance of my daughter, Marian. There are not many survivors left and it becomes more important to educate people about all the atrocities, which happened during that time. It is so crucial to inform people in the hope that it will never be repeated. I feel privileged to still be able to do this.

After all the years of writing my memoirs, I wish to end this while thinking of all my children, grandchildren and great-grandchildren and future unborn offspring. I wrote this for you with the prayers and the hope that all of you live a life, which is good, productive, kind and full of love and respect. Respect for your fellow human beings will make you a better person. If you have respect for every one you come in contact with, life will be so much easier and the world will be a better place.

"Sometimes I am asked about Revenge. My personal revenge is sweet: To live a good, productive life, to have four children, eleven grandchildren and currently seventeen great grandchildren is very special and something the nazies never wanted to have happen. I am so very grateful."
—Carla Olman Peperzak, April 2018

"The Holocaust is part of my life. I'm formed by it. I, like most people, try to see the best in people," Carla Peperzak said, turning to what she wants her children, grandchildren and great-grandchildren to know.

For a long time, she never talked about her experiences, only telling her children that her relatives had died in the Holocaust.

She taught them never to throw food away; be good people and good neighbors; be open minded; do not hate; respect other people's viewpoints, and accept others for who they are.

"If we can respect each other, our points of view and our religions, what a wonderful world it would be. Respect is the most important word in the vocabulary," she said.

After her children became adults, she began telling them more. When her granddaughters were eight and 10, Carla went to their class with her daughter. It was the first time they heard her talk about her experiences.

"I wish I had raised my children Jewish, but after the war I didn't want anything to do with Judaism because of my fear and my desire to stay alive," Carla said.

"Yom Hashoah is not just for the Jewish community but for the whole community. We need to care so it won't happen again," she said."

—Fig Tree (April 2011) in Dutch woman taught her children lessons to prevent the Holocaust from being repeated.

http://www.thefigtree.org/april11/040111peperzak.html

Carla in 2018 with Gonzaga Prep students at one of the many presentations she does on the Holocaust for elementary, high school and university students.

Student Letters

The following are just a few of the letters from students, teachers and community members who have attended presentations by Carla Olman Peperzak.

"Listening to [Carla] talk about what she went through and how she was able to help people just really inspired me to stand up against injustice."
—Elsa, student at Freeman High School

"I loved hearing you speak about your life during the Holocaust. It was so cool to hear that you helped so many people and saved so many lives. Your story was really inspiring and I hope I can help people like you did one day. Thank you so much for coming and telling us your story."
—Andy Gadd, Horizon Middle School, 2017

"I just wanted to thank you for visiting my eighth grade English class. It meant so much to me, and to all of us. We truly are grateful to have heard your story. It was eye opening and heartbreaking for me personally. It is something that I will always try to remember. The emotion in your voice moved me in an unexplainable way. It touched my heart, and for that, I can never thank you enough.

The knowledge you have given me from that period of time will stay with me forever. I will apply it to everyday life as much as I can. If it's as simple as being kind to someone, even if I don't like him or her, I will do it. What I took away from that experience was that we should all learn to accept each other and that some people are just mad. They cannot accept people for who they are, and that is something I will always pride myself in doing. Accepting. Your story showed me that. It taught me so many things I don't think I'd be able to fit it on a single page, and I don't want to bother, bore, or tire you with the reasons, but I will say it once more. Thank you, Carla."

—Jena Austin, River City Middle School March 25, 2013

"Carla's story is a testament to the fact that we are headed in the right direction, that I am a part of something greater than myself."

—SSgt Airman, Anna Archer

"Thank you so much for coming to our class to speak about your experiences with the Dutch Resistance during World War II. It was fascinating to hear about what life was like within the historical events we learn about. You were very brave, and you are very kind to share that with us. The original documents were wonderful to see as well. Again, thank you very much for coming in. We really appreciate it!

—Gail Gallaher, West Valley High School 2013

"Mrs. Peperzak's visit was really incredible. It is difficult to share traumatic events, the fact she was willing to share this part of her life was really amazing and a once in a lifetime opportunity (given most of these survivors are at the end of their lives). During a lot of my travels I never gained the insight to other people's opinions of WW2 – only the German's. This was a unique perspective for me, and one I really valued. I value it because it shows amazing strength in the face of adversity. It shows that even if something is difficult you should do the right thing. It is very humbling.

During Christmas it is very common to see people act kinder to one another, and show more interest in other people's lives and wellbeing. This generally disappears after April (maybe due to tax season). These stories need to be told. Not so much as the idea that we should know what extent hatred like Nazism can lead to, but so we will act. I think that point is missed sometimes when American or even European students hear "never again."

—Student of Dr. Raymond Sun, December 2015

"Thank you for coming to speak in our class. You were a huge inspiration to us all. You showed us all the importance of standing up for justice."
—Sam, Gonzaga University student

"To me, denying the Holocaust is ridiculous. As a witness to this time, I can imagine that statements like these must make you very angry. So many people (Jews and non-Jews) suffered immensely. The Holocaust really shows the dark side of the human heart. It shows how hate can spread like a virus. However, the fact those resistances formed almost immediately shows that there are people who know what is right and are willing to fight for it. I think that the people who stood up to the Nazis during that time are truly the bravest, because today many people say they would fight back but really wouldn't. You cannot know the real measure of your bravery until you are faced with the question of life and death.
—Claire Forsberg, River City Middle School, 2013

"Thank you so much for coming and speaking to our class. Your story is amazing and I have never heard anything like it. You have inspired me to learn more about the Holocaust and talk to people about it. The part of your speech that left me most impacted was when you said you lived every day in fear. That seems obvious, but I'd never thought about that, and I cannot even begin to imagine what that must have been like."
—Maddy, Gonzaga University student

"I have been fortunate enough to listen to four other Holocaust survivors in my life time. Hearing the different experiences between each person who has survived the Holocaust. I learn something new every time. I loved hearing what you said about Pearl Harbor. I've never heard of anyone speaking of it as such a relief, but having that understanding means a lot to me. Also, my grandfather was in Norway during World War II and he has only been able to speak to me once about how he was involved. He gets emotional and like you, just wants to forget. I hope that I can tell him about you and inspire him to tell more people about his experiences. Again, thank you Carla."

—Marit, Gonzaga University student

"I want to personally thank you for coming to our school. Your speech was tremendously educational and I am lucky that I was able to hear it. Most kids will never get this experience in their lifetime. It was incredible how you were able to make me see a glimpse at what happened almost 70 years ago. The way you told the stories from your point of view could never be found in any history book.

You are very inspiring because of your bravery at only 16. If I were put into that situation, I would not have reacted that way. You had every opportunity to be safe and you risked it to help others. In my perspective that is what a true here does. How you talked made me really engaged and wanting to learn more. The history books we get in class don't even compare to the hour and a half speech you gave. I learned more in those few hours than I did in an entire

2 months. I took so many notes when you were speaking because I want to remember this day forever. So I want to thank you again for giving me this experience that I will remember for a lifetime."
—Hannah Reinhart, Horizon Middle School, 2016

"Thinking about what you want through and what you may have seen shows me that you are a very strong and brave human being. I truly do admire what you did and I think people in this time should be more respectful of it. It is my personal belief that there will always be people with hate in their hearts, to this day there is human trafficking, slavery and hate of other religions I fell like everybody has at least experienced some sort of hate against them. The holocaust is probably the most remembered genocide there is but it will certainly not be the last. I truly do hope that we will someday never have to experience this again. I would truly like to thank you for everything you did and for telling us about your life and decisions when you were only a teenager. Thank you so much."
—Ashlyn Tidwell, Horizon Middle School, 2016

"Thank you very much for coming to speak with us. It means a lot that you would take the time to travel to the school and tell us about this sensitive subject. I understand the Holocaust can be very difficult to talk about. And I deeply appreciate that you tell your story still. I admire you very much and I hope you know that. Your bravery is more than I could ever fathom. Saving lives at the age of 17! Yet, through all of your fear, you managed to rescue many people. It pains me to know

that genocides like the Holocaust still occur. But maybe, if we can get past everyone's differences, we can prevent genocides you truly are an inspiration, and you have inspired me. Thank you for that. Thank you for giving each of us a little more courage to face our fears and make the world a better place. Thank you."
—Lauren Welch, Garfield Middle School, April 2016

"I find your story about the holocaust very inspiring and it has given me a different view on the whole thing. All that I had heard about was life within the camps and how hard it was for the people shipped to the camps. Your story about life outside of the camp and helping with the war effort gave me and idea of life outside of the population stories."
—Isaiah, Gonzaga University student

"First I would like to say thank you for sharing your amazing story with us. It's so easy to look back on history and only see the bad, the hate, but there is so much more and your story is a good reminder of the good, the courage that is there too. When I was little I remember that Mr. Rogers said to look for the helpers whenever there is a tragedy because there will always be helpers. I am so proud to know so many helpers in my life. I am so thankful for the people like you that make the world beautiful in the face of everything that is bad about humanity.
Thank you for being a helper."
—Ellen Wilkey, West Valley High School, 2013

"November 9th of this year is a date that I will never forget. Carla Peperzak, a veteran of the Dutch Resistance and a woman who rescued others during the Holocaust, did much more than tell her story and educate our class on the civilian resistance during WWII. Mrs. Peperzak showed pictures of her loved ones, shared how they lived, died, or have since passed on. She trusted us with old and important documents such as fake identification cards for Jews. Before leaving us, Mrs. Peperzak told us to remember to always be kind and respectful towards our fellow human. It was clear that if she could sacrifice and risk so much to help others, that we could also do something to make the world a more positive and loving place. In our hands we held history and in her words we heard the future.

Mrs. Peperzak's message resonated with me in more than one way. Clearly her comments regarding loving one another and respect were important and moving, but also it was her courage that changed my perception of what courageous really means. While it is undeniable that the men who fought during this war showed strength and determination, that was their job. They were trained, prepared, and had reinforcements. Someone else was calling the shots, and they had well thought out plans. Mrs. Peperzak was a young girl who was figuring out her resistance techniques as she went, and risking her and her families' safety every day. While I sat and listened to her speak, I couldn't help but wonder if I personally would have the courage to do what she had done, to risk my life to save others. I pray to never see myself in a situation such as hers, but if that ever were the case I hope to make a difference." —Gonzaga University student

"The students were absolutely enthralled. I wish they were better at asking questions. The letters are sweet. I would call you brilliant!"
—Jerri Sheppard, Gonzaga University Professor

"Thank you for coming and presenting to our World War II history class last week. This was actually the second time I was able to hear your story as you spoke to my class last spring that was focused on researching Holocaust rescue and resistance. However, I never took the opportunity to write to you and express my appreciation for what you do. I know there is sacrifice involved—travelling is always tiring, and you have earned your right to live a retired life! Secondly, I could not imagine it would be easy to talk about these things and constantly relive the fear, anxiety, sorrow, and stress of this time in your life. Even so, you present yourself so professionally and speak so calmly and eloquently. I am so impressed with your ability to convey these difficult experiences of your life with such composure.

I am currently in the process of getting my Masters in Teaching. My student teaching placement is in a middle school in Clarkston, WA—not exactly an affluent place. When kids struggle to read and have very little knowledge of the broader world, teaching them about history (or getting them interested in it in general) can be a real challenge. I believe that one of the keys to engaging them and helping them understand difficult historical concepts is teaching history through individual stories. I believe in the power of individual stories because of how they help me process, grasp, and remember history myself. One of the most difficult concepts in history for anyone to grasp is that of genocide and how it happens (or is allowed to happen). Even after taking multiple classes on the Holocaust, I struggle to understand it as well.

That is where sharing a personal narrative is so much more powerful than the omniscient voice of a textbook. It is so important to hear from the perspective of someone who lived through it. It is important to hear that your own friends from the rowing group were taken in a Nazi roundup, because the listener then can conceptualize their own friends being taken. It is important to see pictures taken of your family sitting by Nazi soldiers because it is far easier to understand the daily stress of avoiding discovery of your true identity and associations. Something I began to better understand about Holocaust rescue is that which makes those involved so courageous is not simply the exciting stories of confronting Nazi officers, lying under pressure, so on and so forth. Choosing to resist meant choosing to live in constant danger of being discovered. I think that small revelation is important for us all to understand so that, if put in a similar situation, we are more mentally prepared. Too often we look at the bystanders of the Holocaust with such judgment, but if we want to prevent something like this from happening again, we have to be aware of the costs involved.

I wrote some of your closing words in my notes—
"even if you don't like or understand them, if you
respect your fellow human, you cannot kill." In my
future as a teacher, I will undoubtedly teach about the
Holocausts and other genocides in history. I will likely
have conversations with my students about the
ongoing atrocities in the world. I think that quote will be
immensely helpful in explaining these kinds of things
and in answering the inevitable question of "how do we
prevent it from happening again?"

Thank you for your commitment to education and
awareness on this topic. In a world where there are so
many bad things that are ultimately beyond our
control, you are a powerful example of doing what you
can do make a difference within your community and
personal sphere. Perhaps we can all do more than we
think.

I was honored to meet you and shake your hand."

—Claire Thornton, November 17, 2017

"Thank you so much for coming in and talking to our
class and the people that attended. I did not know
much about the Dutch Resistance, and to hear
someone's first-hand account of their experience in the
resistance was really special to me. I also want to
thank you for your courage in helping those people
that you could; I do not think I would have the courage
to go against an army of Nazi's myself. Loved hearing
you talk, and I hope our paths cross again someday."

—Jake, Gonzaga University student

"My name is Dustin Dennis; you might remember me as the student in the full Army Dress Uniform who listened to your presentation. I wanted to say thank you very much, both for the courage you displayed during World War Two and the courage you must have be able to share your experiences with us of the next generations. By listening to you I gained a far more insightful look at the daily lives of people under Nazi oppression.

As History majors we often forget to look at the small individuals during times of great strife such as you lived through. We look at themes and strategies and other things that almost only show us the big picture. You brought it back down to the person, to how the individual is affecting people's lives. That for me brought up just how often we overlook the small deeds in favor of the large ones.

But the one factor that you did bring forward that I had never really considered before is how you explained your fear of capture during this time. It had never occurred to me that fearing the Germans was not the primary thing on your mind, but the actual fear of other Dutch citizens. You explained to us that the collaborators to the Germans were the ones that you feared most because they were the most likely reason you would get caught. This really opened my eyes to how the way it was under Nazi Oppression. So, I really must thank you again for coming to speak with us here at Washington State University."

—Dustin Dennis, Cadet U.S. Army

Thank you so much for coming in and talking to our class. I am very fascinated in everything you had to talk about. You have an excellent story to be told and I'm sure the whole world would love to hear this, but aren't fortunate enough. I am so glad that I received the opportunity to hear your story."
—Theo, Gonzaga University student

"You are such an inspiring person and you have made such a lasting impact. I don't know if I could have the courage to do the things you did! How you keep on going is something that I cannot fathom. I can't thank you enough. You are so selfless, the way you give your time to teach my generation. Many kids my age won't ever get a chance to meet a survivor, so from the bottom of my heart I greatly thank you."
—Madeline Loy, Horizon Middle School, 2016

"I would like to thank you for coming and speaking to our class. It is very rare that a high-profile speaker like yourself would come and speak to a class that size. Your experience during World War II and the Holocaust were very inspiring and enlightening. I learned a lot from your presentation, it was interesting to hear about The Netherlands during Nazi occupation because it is often a country that is over looked in the history of the Second World War. Prior to your presentation my knowledge of The Netherlands during World War II was very limited, but after listening to you speak, The Netherlands is one of the countries that I have the greatest understanding in regard to life under Nazi occupation. I was amazed to find out that not only did you know Ann Frank but also at one time you lived only a block away from her! During your presentation, it was interesting to find out that Amsterdam had a large and thriving Jewish population, I was unaware of that. After listening to you speak I am very certain that you are a powerful woman with strong moral values. You risked your own life multiple times in order to save those who could not save themselves. In my opinion, the Holocaust is the worst single event to occur during the 20th century. In our class, we have learned that a much greater number of Europeans under Nazi rule aided the evil regime, it was nice to hear more about the resistance and that there were still good individuals during that dark period of history. I can only imagine how hard it is for you to speak on such a dark topic that had such a major impact on your personal life. My great grandfather happened to be a Jew living in Austria at the beginning of Nazi occupation. He was sent to a work camp, but eventually escaped. He was so traumatized by his experience during the Holocaust that he did not speak about it until the 1980's. I believe that it is extremely important that stories like your own are told, so not only to remember the terrible atrocities that people went through, but also to also identify and stop any similar situations from ever happening again. Ms. Peperzak you are truly a hero and I would like to thank you again for taking time out of your day to come speak to Dr. Sun's class, elohim yevarex otax."

—Michael (Mick) Thompson, November 14, 2017

"To begin, I would like to say thank you for taking the time to talk with us on Thursday. Your unique experiences are not only inspiring but they were captivating to learn about. After your presentation, I was the first to talk with you about my experience in Holland and about my family on my Father's side originating from Breukelen, The Netherlands. My last name is Van Brocklin and when you heard that, I found it very funny when you said "well that definitely makes it easy". I will not forget meeting you, as it was a once in a lifetime chance to meet you!

Your stories were also very impactful to our class. Having first-hand accounts gives the history of World War II a more personal reality rather than a textbook one. Learning how things were for you during those times was interesting to me, as well as your story on how the Dutch Resistance acquired various things from the British through codes like "it looks as if this one area will be getting rain tonight." One question I had was if the Resistance had any information on the Death Camps before the war ended. I know the SS kept the death camps top secret but I was not sure if the Resistance ever received any knowledge from sources. Besides my question, learning more about how the war was in Amsterdam and elsewhere was very intriguing. Thank you again for saving the 40 lives that you did and for coming to talk to our little class."

—Brent Van Brocklin, Professor Sun's class Nov 14th, 2017

"Thank you for coming to speak to our class on November 9th. It was an honor to hear about your experiences as a Holocaust rescuer/survivor and your role as a Dutch resistance fighter during WWII. I was

amazed by some of the stories you told us, especially the story you told about rescuing your nephew who was aboard a train that was headed to a concentration camp. You were willing to risk your life to save as many people as possible from a horrible fate. Thank you for standing up against the Nazi regime and for standing up against hate, and thank you for fighting for your country. After your presentation, you have inspired me to be a better person, and have inspired me to help people who are in need. Thank you again for taking the time to speak for our class. It was an honor and a privilege to hear you speak, and it was an honor to meet you."
—Becky Shank

"I am so inspired by your story. Growing up I have loved learning about history and I never had the chance to be able to listen to someone from the past and who experienced one of the moments in history I am so interested in. I really enjoyed your presentation. You have opened my eyes to another side to the story. "Respect" I know is something I will carry with me.
—Student

"Hearing about your life was such an amazing treat for our class today. It was so interesting to hear about your stories. You are a truly inspirational person. You are so brave and heroic. I'm sure your entire family looks up to you as much as we already did."
—Sam, Gonzaga University student

"Thank you for sharing your story with our class. It is not often people our age get to listen to firsthand experiences from such a historical time in the world. It's hard to fathom everything that went on around WWII, but you do a great job articulating the events and personal experiences. It is truly appreciated."

—Peter, Gonzaga University student

"Thank you so much for not only speaking to our class, but thank you for sharing your story. It was incredibly inspiring and your bravery is amazing. Being so young you chose to put your life in danger for others. That really spoke to me and I admire you greatly. I feel honored to even have been in the same room with you. It was a blessing hearing from you. Thank you for your bravery!"

—Mari, Gonzaga University student

"Hearing your presentation was both moving and shocking. You shed a new light on the Holocaust for me. I studied the French Resistance in high school but never the Dutch. It's incredible not only what you did, but that you share your story. You remind me that it's always important to stand up for what you believe in, and to never let people forget something like that. Thank you for your time and your courage."

—Jordan, Gonzaga University student

"I wanted to say thank you for coming to Gonzaga. It was fascinating to hear your story. I cannot think of the amount of courage and bravery it took to be in the Resistance. I take pride in your words to make a better

world. To spread respect would create such a wonderful world. Again, thank you so much for coming in."
—Taylor, Gonzaga University student

"It's truly amazing to hear you share your story. I went to Freeman High School and although I was unable to hear you speak, the power of your message and story quickly spread through the halls of our small school. I find you to be a very strong woman for the courage you show every day by sharing your experiences and for helping those in need even when your life is at risk as well."
—McKabe, Gonzaga University student

"My name is Brandon Jones, a senior at WSU, and I am majoring in Neuroscience and History. I will keep it short, as I am sure you will be receiving a lot of feedback. A little about myself: I spent eight years serving as a Fleet Marine Force Corpsman (providing emergency medical treatment to Marines). I was deployed twice; once to Iraq, and the other to Afghanistan. To date, I have lost 31 brothers due to combat, or from suicide from psychological wounds sustained following our deployments. I still suffer from both deployments, but always try to find the best in life to keep me going. Throughout my time in the service, I was fortunate enough to have met genuine heroes of this world. Upon reading about you, and listening to you speak; I am proud to say that I have met another hero. What you did for your country, and for the well being of humanity, is nothing short of miraculous.

Unlike many in life, I never idolize celebrities, but I do idolize people that truly make a difference in the world. You are one of those difference makers. If, by the time I am your age, I have accomplished half of what you have in life, my life will be successful. Thank you for sharing your story, and most importantly, thank you for all you have done in life. In a world surrounded by selfishness, you are the inspiration we all need; a person we all should strive to become. I will never forget your story. From the bottom of my heart, thank you!"

—Brandon Jones

"Thank you for taking time out of your day to come talk to us about the Holocaust and your experiences in the Holocaust. I thought that your story was inspiring being as how you did all those astonishing acts of bravery, such as printing off fake passports and just saving all of those people in general and how you didn't let the fear overtake you. Once again thank you for taking time out of your day to come talk to us and being the hero you are."

—Tristan West, Garfield Middle School, April 2016

"Last Tuesday, I had the honor of sponsoring Senate Resolution 8623 which recognizes a Spokane hero, Carla Peperzak. Carla, who has lived in Spokane since 2004, served in the Dutch Resistance as a teenager during Nazi occupation. With courage and selflessness, Carla helped dozens of families."
—Sen. Andy Billig, Washington State Senate Democrat March 2015.

Senator Billig presenting Carla Peperzak with a copy of Senate Resolution 8623 recognizing her as a Spokane Hero. "Carla is a person of incredible grace and heroism. I'd like her story told as far and wide as possible." — Sen. Andy Billig, D-Spokane.

Resources

"When Nazis invaded her home in Amsterdam, Carla Peperzak's Jewish father was able to provide papers to prove that Carla and her sisters were born of a Catholic mother, saving them from incarceration. Carla joined the Dutch resistance, saving 40 Jews by providing food and shelter and helping to falsify IDs. Carla grew up in Amsterdam, the daughter of a Jewish father and Catholic mother. When the Nazis invaded Holland, Carla's father was able to acquire papers that identified Carla, her sister, and mother as non-Jewish. With this freedom, Carla joined the Dutch resistance. Her efforts, including falsifying IDs and obtaining food and shelter for Jews in hiding, helped save about forty people. Carla resides in Spokane and joined the Holocaust Center Speakers Bureau in 2014."

—Holocaust Survivor Carla Peperzak at The Holocaust Center for Humanity Lunch-and-Learn
https://www.thestranger.com/events/26179053/holocaust-survivor-carla-peperzak-lunch-and-learn

"In addition to a amazing first person account of Holocaust, Mrs. Perperzak provided the key take away point regarding the importance of Respect. She presented during Community Period today."

—Gonzaga Preparatory School in Spokane, Washington
With the theme of Resilience several speakers are on campus including Carla Peperzak.
https://www.gprep.com/apps/news/article/809364

"Carla Peperzak was 16 when the German occupation started in her native Holland in the spring of 1940. She was 18 when she first helped a family go into hiding.

She became a U.S. citizen in 1958 and moved to Spokane in 2004, often speaking publicly about her experiences in schools to educate today's children about the Holocaust.

"I did not have any responsibility – only for myself – and that made a big difference. I felt I could help. I had the opportunity," Peperzak told The Spokesman-Review in 2015.

Peperzak will be a guest panelist at Coffee Talk: Forgive or Forget at 10 a.m. Saturday (Aug. 5) at the Saranac Commons, 19 W Main Ave. Other panelists were SpokaneFāVS writers Patricia Bruininks, who teaches psychology at Whitworth, poet Christi Ortiz and guest panelist Melissa Opel of the Spokane Buddhist Temple."

—Carla Peperzak, who helped hide Jews during the Holocaust, Coffee Talk panelist

https://spokanefavs.com/carla-peperzak-who-helped-hide-jews-during-the-holocaust-added-as-coffee-talk-panelist/

"When I talk to schools, I always end with the word respect," Peperzak said. "Because I think if one can learn to respect one another, you can't kill."

Peperzak was finishing her final high school exams when the Nazis invaded her home country in May 1940. The family was forced to register as Jewish, obtaining ID cards and a yellow "Star of David" patch to wear on their coats – for which Dutch Jews had to pay 15 cents. Her Jewish father's clothing factory was seized by authorities.

"Everything was stolen," Peperzak said. "And, of course, we couldn't go to the police."

Peperzak joined the Dutch resistance, or "the Underground," after her father was able to register the rest of her family as non-Jewish. She spent the war forging identification papers and ration cards, pedaling on her bicycle to assist friends and family in hiding and huddling in closets with stolen radios to receive news uncensored by the Nazis that she would then reprint and circulate in pamphlets.

Peperzak's parents and sister knew nothing of her resistance work, said her daughter, Marian Cummings.

"They did not share with each other what they were doing," Cummings said. Peperzak's sister, Whilemina, focused on securing food so the family could eat, while Peperzak bartered stolen sugar for new bicycle tires so she could get around to the families she was helping.

Once, a pair of Nazi secret police interrogated Peperzak, she said. Finding nothing out of order, the agents offered to help her carry a briefcase out of her home – a case containing forged paperwork and the machinery necessary to manufacture it.

"If it had opened, by chance, I wouldn't be sitting here," Peperzak said.

The experiences rocked her faith. Immediately after the war, Peperzak said she "wanted nothing to do with Judaism," but has since returned to the religion. She can't forgive the Nazis for killing millions, but the hate has left her heart after all these years.

— Holocaust Survivor and Member of the Dutch Resistance Movement Carla Peperzak in Spokesman Review Friday, Oct. 20, 2017.
http://www.spokesman.com/stories/2017/oct/21/holocaust-freedom-fighter-carla-peperzak-preaches-/#/0

"Carla Peperzak grew up in Amsterdam, the daughter of a Jewish father and Catholic mother. When the Nazis invaded Holland, Carla, like other Jews, had to register to have her identification card branded with a "J," but Carla's father was able to acquire papers that identified Carla, her sister, and mother as non-Jewish. With this freedom, Carla joined the Dutch resistance. She stole a German ID and bought a German nurse's uniform and, with this disguise, she traveled, securing hiding places for Jews in rural Holland. She brought them food, medical supplies, and forged papers. Her efforts helped save about forty people. Carla joined the Holocaust Center's Speakers Bureau in 2014. She resides in Spokane, WA and is the last known survivor sharing her story there."

—Carla Peperzak: Holocaust Survivor & Member of the Dutch Resistance Sep 18, 2017. YouTube Video. https://www.youtube.com/watch?v=fHnq1ZNRirs

"It's an amazing story she is sharing today," said Col. Ryan Samuelson, 92nd Air Refueling Wing commander. "We're honored that she has taken the time to tell her story and help us clearly remember the tragedies that happened at the hands of Nazi Germany."

—WWII Survivor shares her story at Fairchild Air Force Base April 25, 2017.
http://www.fairchild.af.mil/News/Article-Display/Article/1162406/wwii-survivor-shares-her-story/

"Our featured speaker, Carla Peperzak, will talk about her experiences in the Dutch Resistance during World War II, a time when many were being persecuted. Mrs. Peperzak gives us an opportunity to look at the past and move forward in hope and respect for one another."

—Task Force sponsors Human Rights Day Sandpoint Reader, Dec 7, 2017. http://sandpointreader.com/task-force-sponsors-human-rights-day/

Trustee: Carla O. Peperzak and Marcus B. Peperzak. The Council of National Trustees acts as an ambassador for National Jewish Health. The trustees help organize events, raise funds and spread the word about our institution – in their own communities throughout the country.

—National Jewish Health: Council of National Trustees. https://www.nationaljewish.org/about/leadership/trustees

"Three Sandpoint High School students from the Model UN class will present a brief history and development of the Universal Declaration of Human Rights. Following the students' presentation, our featured speaker, Mrs. Carla Peperzak, will talk about her experiences in the Dutch Resistance during World War II, a time when many were being persecuted."

—Bonner County Day Pays Tribute to Human Rights, Dec 8, 2017. http://www.bonnercountydailybee.com/lifestyles/20171208/day_pays_tribute_to_human_rights

Carla Peperzak, local educator and Holocaust survivor nominated to the Spokane Citizen Hall of Fame's Education category in 2016. https://www.inlander.com/Bloglander/archives/2016/03/08/ finalists-announced-for-spokane-citizen-hall-of-fames-2016-inductee-class

Carla Peperzak came to speak to our 7th and 8th grade students on May 21st. She was a survivor of the Holocaust.

She was born in 1923 in Holland. She grew up in Amsterdam right across the street from Anne Frank. Carla was never sent to a concentration camp, she was part of the resistance.

"The accomplishments Carla made when she was young are just remarkable. She is one woman that I would consider a hero!" — A MLMS Student when Carla was a Medical Lake Middle School Speaker. https://mlms.mlsd.org/apps/news/article/872897

"Listening to [Carla] talk about what she went through and how she was able to help people just really inspired me to stand up against injustice," said Elsa, student at Freeman High School. Carla Peperzak is a survivor who helped rescue around 40 Jews as a member of the Dutch Resistance. —She shares her story as a member of the Seattle Holocaust Center Speakers' Bureau. https://www.holocaustcenterseattle.org/join-and-give/voices-for-humanity

"A Spokane great-grandmother will be honored in Olympia next week for her work as a teenage Dutch Resistance operative during World War II.

Carla Olman Peperzak, 91, helped hide approximately 40 Jews from the Germans. She also forged identification papers, served as a messenger and helped publish a newsletter for the underground movement.

"Carla is a person of incredible grace and heroism. I'd like her story told as far and wide as possible," said Sen. Andy Billig, D-Spokane.

This May marks the 70th anniversary of the end of World War II in Europe.

"There will be a time soon when there will be nobody left who was alive during this terrible period of our history, and that history has to be preserved even after they are gone," Billig said. "One of the ways we can memorialize and remember the terror of the Nazi regime – and also the heroism of those who opposed it – is to shine as bright a light as possible on the people that can best share those stories."

—Spokane woman to be honored for role in WWII Dutch Resistance. March 6, 2015 Spokesman-Review. http://www.spokesman.com/stories/2015/mar/06/spokane-woman-to-be-honored-for-role-in-wwii/

"Spokane's Carla Olman Peperzak, 91, shares her amazing story as a wartime Dutch Resistance operative and Holocaust survivor. By her own estimation, Carla helped hide 40 Jews from the Germans during World War II;

forged identification papers for about five dozen others; served as a messenger for the Underground movement; and helped publish a newsletter of Allied Forces' activities on a banned mimeograph machine. This very special program includes a video screening of the documentary "With My Own Eyes," which provides historical context and shares the stories of other Northwest holocaust survivors."

—Carla Peperzak: Her Real-Life Story Protecting Jews as a Dutch Resistance Operative on Spokane 7.
http://www.spokane7.com/calendar/events/55955/158858/

"Last Tuesday, I had the honor of sponsoring Senate Resolution 8623 which recognizes a Spokane hero, Carla Peperzak. Carla, who has lived in Spokane since 2004, served in the Dutch Resistance as a teenager during Nazi occupation. With courage and selflessness, Carla helped dozens of families."

—Sen. Andy Billig – Washington State Senate Democrats Mar 26, 2015.

http://sdc.wastateleg.org/billig/2015/03/17/e-newsletter-honoring-a-spokane-hero/

"Carla Peperzak, a survivor and Dutch resistance member during the occupation of Holland by Nazi Germany, accepts commemorative coins and flowers from Col. Ryan Samuelson, 92nd Air Refueling Wing commander, Apr. 24, 2017, at Fairchild Air Force Base,

Wash. At 91 years old, Peperzak is the last known holocaust survivor in the Spokane area." Fairchild Air Force Base Speaker. https://www.alamy.com/carla-peperzak-a-survivor-and-dutch-resistance-member-during-the-occupation-of-holland-by-nazi-germany-accepts-commemorative-coins-and-flowers-from-col-ryan-samuelson-92nd-air-refueling-wing-commander-apr-24-2017-at-fairchild-air-force-base-wash-at-91-years-old-peperzak-is-the-last-known-holocaust-survivor-in-the-spokane-area-image187230434.html

"The featured speaker is Carla Peperzak, a member of the Dutch resistance who has firsthand experience of how she and others resisted the Holocaust."
—KRFY Radio | Civic Events Apr 8, 2015.
http://www.krfy.org/civic-events/

"Carla Olman Peperzak donned a blue-and-white nurse's uniform and made her way to Amsterdam's Central Station. She had received word that an aunt and five cousins would be passing through on the way to Westerbork, the Nazi detention center in northeast Holland. Her uncle had already been seized by the Nazis. So when Peperzak found her relatives in a railcar waiting on the tracks she asked if she could take the youngest one. She carried the toddler off the train. But the station was teeming with German soldiers, and a couple of them stopped her. Who are you and where are you going, they wanted to know. Peperzak was a teenage wartime Dutch Resistance operative who, by her estimation, helped hide approximately 40 Jews from the Germans during World War II. She forged identification papers for about five dozen others, served as a messenger for the Underground movement and helped publish a newsletter of Allied Forces' activities on a banned mimeograph machine.

These are not the things she told the Nazis.

In German, which she had learned in school as well as from her Austrian nanny, Peperzak said the boy was sick and needed to get to a hospital. She was young, attractive and Jewish. She was also disguised as a German nurse, with a stolen medical identification card in her pocket. If her true identity had been discovered, "That would have been the end of me."

Still, she didn't consider herself particularly brave. Her resistance was born of gratitude. Peperzak didn't wear a star. So she helped those who did.

"I was 18, 19, and 20. I was not married. I did not have any responsibility – only for myself – and that made a big difference," she said. "I felt I could help. I had the opportunity."

—Freedom fighter: Spokane's Carla Peperzak protected fellow Jews through Dutch Resistance during World War II Sun., Jan. 25, 2015 Spokesman Review. http://www.spokesman.com/stories/2015/jan/25/freedom-fighter/

"Carla joined the underground movement when her father's brother asked her to help him, his wife and two children hide. She asked a neighbor she trusted to help her find a place for them. After that, she was in the network.

Carla Peperzak, who helped family and strangers, displays copies of her ID card and ration cards on her desk.

They needed new IDs. So Carla began helping the resistance prepare IDs. Forms printed in England were dropped at night in fields by small, low-flying planes, piloted or navigated by Dutch people who had fled to England. They knew the countryside. By radio, they arranged the airdrops.

"We took people's pictures in photo machines on the streets. I had a machine to make thumbprints and an official seal. We changed people's names, keeping their initials in case they had a ring or handkerchief with initials. I made new ID cards before people went into hiding. Some who did not look Jewish used the cards and did not go into hiding.

Carla knew if she was caught, she would be shot or taken to a concentration camp.

"I was young, as most in the underground and I did not think a lot about that," she said. "I was grateful not to have a 'J' on my ID, and I wanted to help people."

—Dutch Underground Risked Their Own Safety to Protect Others April 2013 Fig Tree.
http://www.thefigtree.org/april13/040113peperzak.html

Ms. Peperzak was the guest speaker prior to the performance of The Diary of Anne Frank as presented by the North Idaho College Theatre Department.

— North Idaho College - Carla Peperzak, Nazi Resistor on YouTube Nov 11, 2013.

https://www.youtube.com/watch?v=gSjJj5nwT6M

"The Holocaust is part of my life. I'm formed by it. I like most people and try to see the best in people," Carla said, turning to what she wants her children, grandchildren and great grandchildren to know.

For a long time, she never talked about her experiences, only telling her children that her relatives had died in the Holocaust.

She taught them never to throw food away; be good people and good neighbors; be open minded; do not hate; respect other people's viewpoints, and accept others for who they are.

"If we can respect each other, our points of view and our religions, what a wonderful world it would be. Respect is the most important word in the vocabulary," she said.

After her children became adults, she began telling them more. When her granddaughters were eight and 10, Carla went to their class with her daughter. It was the first time they heard her talk about her experiences.

She has only gone a few times to schools to tell her story. Once, she spoke to the cast of "The Diary of Anne Frank" at Central Valley High school. She has also talked at Temple Beth Shalom and at her Rockwood community.

"I wish I had raised my children Jewish, but after the war I didn't want anything to do with Judaism because of my fear and my desire to stay alive," Carla said.

"Yom Hashoah is not just for the Jewish community but for the whole community. We need to care so it won't happen again," she said.

Dutch woman taught her children lessons to prevent the Holocaust from being repeated April 2011 FigTree. http://www.thefigtree.org/april11/040111peperzak.html

"I was always worried," said Holocaust survivor Carla Peperzak. "I was always afraid. You never knew what would happen from one time to the next."

Peperzak spoke to about 75 students, faculty and community members Wednesday, April 13, in the Jundt Art Center's Charlotte Y. Martin Foundation Lecture Hall as part of this year's Holocaust memorial service.

The service, which took place in anticipation of the upcoming Jewish Holocaust remembrance day Yom Hashoah, after brief introductions by the event's organizers, LGBT Resource Center Coordinator Ryan King and religious studies professor Dr. Elizabeth Goldstein.

Peperzak, a neighbor of Anne Frank, was a Jewish teenager living in Amsterdam during World War II. She described how the war years were permeated by fear as she worked in the underground army to find hiding places for Jewish friends and family members.

Amsterdam had one of the largest Jewish populations of any western European city, according to Peperzak. There were about 70,000 Jews living in Amsterdam prior to the war. By 1945, there were 20,000.

"The Germans were very severe and very thorough in catching the Jewish people," she said.

Peperzak described how initially she was given an ID card with a "J" next to her picture, along with a yellow Star of David patch, which she held up for the audience to see.

However, her father foresaw the danger and consulted with an attorney to have Peperzak and her siblings issued new IDs without the "J," since her mother grew up Catholic.

After that, she said, "I was free to go. I felt that I could walk in the streets."

Peperzak then became involved with the Jewish resistance. She helped search for hiding places and procured ration cards to feed concealed Jews. British planes would drop paper forms at night and Peperzak said she became adept at printing false ID cards.

She also carried codes from one place to another.

"Only one time I was stopped," Peperzak said. The Germans wanted to confiscate her bicycle. "I talked them out of it."

She recounted how she had friends and relatives who were taken to the Nazi concentration camps. Many resisted but there were some, like Peperzak's uncle, who were averse to hiding and felt that "if God wants me to go, then I'll go."

In one instance, someone informed Peperzak that her aunt and cousins were being taken away on a train. Peperzak managed to free her youngest cousin, but her aunt and the others were never heard from again, she said.

Sophomore Sal Schifano said this story made him feel "challenged to do something meaningful with my life. By the time [Peperzak] was 18, she had already saved multiple people's lives."

—Holocaust survivor speaks on campus by Stephen Paur / Staff Writer, Gonzaga Bulletin Apr 18, 2011 https://www.gonzagabulletin.com/article_c8856eca-8f8a-569e-b059-09cdabcdf05d.html.

Carla Olman Peperzak in 2018.

About the Author

Carla was born and raised in Amsterdam, The Netherlands. She was sixteen years old in 1940 when the nazies occupied The Netherlands. She is a Holocaust survivor and persevered for three and a half years as an active resistance fighter in the Dutch Resistance. Mainly Carla helped fellow Jews in hiding.

She met and married her husband, Paul, after the war. She first arrived in the U.S. in 1948. She and Paul lived on several continents. They moved 13 times overseas and in the U.S. Carla moved to Spokane in 2004 following Paul's death. During the last 10 years she has dedicated her life to educating people about the Holocaust mainly to students at middle schools, high schools and universities primarily in the Pacific Inland Northwest. She is an official speaker of the Seattle based Holocaust Institute for Humanity. Carla is passionate in teaching people about the Holocaust so that the atrocities of those years will not be repeated and that the six million Jews who died will not be forgotten. She was honored in 2015 by the state of Washington in the Senate Resolution 8623 as a hero and a person who saved many lives.

Carla considers herself a "professional volunteer" as over the years she has received many awards for her endeavors. Her awards and service includes: President of the World Bank Volunteer Service, President of the Colorado Opera Festival, Recipient of the El Paso County Bar Auxiliary (Molly Walker Award) for outstanding service to law related education, member of the planning group of Opera America Trustee Volunteer Project, Paul and Carla received the award, Opera Guilds International Partners in Excellence, for outstanding volunteer services in the field of Opera, President of the Colorado Opera Festival, Vice-President of Colorado Springs Hadassah Chapter and President of the Spokane Hadassah Chapter, in Kenya she was involved in the Red Cross and organized a scouting troop in Thailand and numerous civic volunteer works.

Carla has become a cornerstone in every one of her communities, naturally helping those in need. She continues to provide time, wisdom, and warmth wherever she can. And, most importantly, as the memory of the Holocaust fades, Carla keeps the flame of remembrance alive for generations to come.

Made in the USA
San Bernardino, CA
20 December 2018